Introduction

IN 1931, a young Army major by the name of George S. Patton, Jr., intrigued with the study of humans in conflict and the effect of leadership on their behavior, authored a text entitled **Success in War.** Within its pages, he wrote:

> *Our means of studying war have increased as much as have our tools for waging it, but it is an open question whether this increase in means has not perhaps obscured or obliterated one essential detail, namely, the necessity for personal leadership.*[1]

Patton had learned through hard experience that technological affluence profits little if an organization is destitute in leadership. Leaders, he knew, are the structural center of a team, the hub around which the organizational wheel is built, and the catalyst to an alchemy of human ingredients, without which the powerful potion known as team cannot be brewed. He went on to build the Third Army, a formidable fighting force whose WWII exploits were feared by the enemy and cheered by Americans at home and overseas.

What was Patton's secret? He was a team-forger—a leader with the ability to fashion individuals into a tool more powerful than the sum of its individual parts. Yet Patton's experience is not unique, nor is the military in sole possession of Patton's wisdom. Pat Riley, former head coach of the Los Angeles Lakers, New York Knickerbockers, and currently with the Miami Heat, has made a career of transforming professional basketball teams from disconnected underperformers to finely tuned, well-orchestrated teams. In **The Winner Within**, Riley tells of his appointment as head coach to a flagging Los Angeles Lakers team in 1981. Though the Lakers' roster read like a Who's Who of basketball luminaries (Kareem Abdul-Jabar, Magic Johnson, James Worthy, *et al.*), they just weren't playing as a team. With the guidance of Coach Riley and the hard work of each member of the team, the Lakers regained their championship form and went on to become a formidable basketball dynasty, ruling the court for most of the 1980s.

Lest we believe that Coach Riley just had a lucky streak, he has proven himself to the task twice more at the professional level. Riley left the Lakers in 1990. After a stint as color commentator, he assumed head coaching duties for the New York Knickerbockers. Again, great players, but no synergy. Under the tutelage of Riley, they became playoff contenders within a year, losing to the Bulls by only a single game. Leaving the Knicks in 1994, he accepted the head coaching position of the Miami Heat, another struggling team. Same story. Within a year, the Heat had become a playoff contender. Resuming coaching duties with the Heat again in 2005, he led them to an NBA championship.

Riley, too, is a team-forger. In **The Winner Within**, he wrote:

> *If there's one thing on which I'm an authority, it's how to blend the talents and strengths of individuals into a force that becomes greater than the sum of its parts. My driving belief is this: great teamwork is the only way to reach our ultimate moments, to create the breakthroughs that define our careers, to fulfill our lives with a sense of lasting significance.*[2]

These are not new words. Any student of leadership reads them again and again, in historical studies as well as modern day recitations of the art called leading. Great leaders in government, business, the armed forces, and sports all learn that distinguished accomplishments come from teams, and superb teams are the reflections of exceptional leaders—leaders who don't just energize teams, but who *synergize* them.

If leadership is so important in building teams, you would assume that the study of leadership would occupy a central position in both the development of potential leaders and the continued refinement of those already in leadership positions. Instead, in most business environments, leadership studies are rarely included, especially for the first line leaders who need them most. Junior leaders are expected either to have or somehow to acquire the necessary characteristics and skills to lead effectively. Indeed, those who have demonstrated expertise as technicians or engineers are frequently thrust into the ranks of leadership in a "sink or swim" fashion which, all too often, results in a drowning. Not only is a team damaged in the process, but a potentially good leader may be set back years in development.

Trustworthy Leaders is a short study in the characteristics and skills shared by effective leaders in business, sports, government, and military endeavors. It draws upon the thoughts of proven leaders, past and present, to identify the attitudes and actions which underlie the development of trust between leaders and team members. The objective of the work is to help bridge the gap for those who have not had the advantage of careful, organized study.

The focus of this work is on age-old leadership principles, traits, and skills rather than some *avant-garde* view of leading. My experiences and studies have convinced me that there is no new or undiscovered method of leading. People are people, and influencing them to accomplish tasks within their respective environments is the crux of leading. Lord Baden-Powell or Juliette Gordon Low, Scouting's founders, would have taught us the same lessons.

Since the ideas themselves are as old as humans and universally applicable to most leadership environments, the illustrations and quotations have been chosen to paint clear images rather than to achieve an artificial balance between races, sexes, or ages. As such, I have not attempted to make this work all things to all people. To have done so would have diluted the content and distracted from the theme. Instead, I have drawn on my own experiences—the same method by which each of us learns to lead—to illustrate the concepts presented in the book. As a result, you will find examples from sports, business, and the military. In that sense, this book is not strictly *business*.

If you are not interested in sports, you may object to the use of sporting examples; yet the development of sports teams offers a unique opportunity to study leadership and its effect in a compressed time frame. To watch Coach Mike Krzyzewski of the Duke Blue Devils or Coach Pat Summitt of Tennessee's Lady Vols lead their teams in college basketball is a fascinating and instructional study in the art of leading. We see leadership in action as these great coaches use forceful behavior when appropriate while, at other times, choosing persuasive, gentle behavior as the most influential tool for the situation.

Similarly, if you have no affiliation with the military community, you may object to the use of martial illustrations. Some believe that there is not a legitimate comparison between leading military organizations and business organizations. My experiences have convinced me differently. I have invested half of my life in military units and half in commercial businesses and have found not a dime's worth of difference between the two. Though the balance between power sources may vary, the principles and techniques necessary to effectively lead people are the same.

Finally, as you proceed in this study, remember that none of us is perfect. We all have committed harmful errors in leading, but, by continuing to study leadership skills, we learn from our errors and become better leaders—at home, at work, in our churches, or wherever we influence others.

H. C. Howlett
President,
TECHSTAR, Inc.

CONTENTS

CONTENTS

LIST OF FIGURES

THE NATURE OF LEADING

- **A Matter of Trust**
- **Character:** A Foundation for Trust
- **Adversity:** The Forge of Character

Leading is an exercise in the acquisition and employment of power, not for the purpose of serving oneself, but for guiding a team toward accomplishment of an objective. The effectiveness of a leader is proportional to the leader's credibility in the eyes of the team. When a leader behaves in a fashion that engenders trust, team members are more likely to follow.

Chapter 1

A MATTER OF TRUST

"We don't willingly follow leaders who are not trustworthy!"

lead•er (lē'dər) *n.* **1.** One that leads or guides. **2.** One who is in charge or in command of others. **3b.** One who has influence or power…

trust (trŭst) *n.* **1.** Firm reliance on the integrity, ability, or character of a person or thing.

LEADERSHIP is the process of influencing people toward achieving goals. Every one of us is a leader. We all influence someone. We are all engaged, consciously or unconsciously, in forming the values of those around us. We are faced, then, with a choice, not of *whether* we will lead, but *how* we will lead.

THE REASON FOR LEADERS

We need strong leaders because accomplishment of complex tasks usually requires multiplication of force through the coordinated and collective efforts of a team of people. If the tasks at hand don't require the efforts of a team, then a leader is probably not necessary.

ROLE OF THE LEADER

The role of the leader is to organize, direct, and harmonize the endeavors of team members toward achieving objectives. Whether orchestra conductor, business team leader, sports coach, or combat commander, most leaders are called upon to blend the efforts of diversely talented team members into synergistic works resulting in mission accomplishment.

As a result, leaders must be multi-talented. We rely upon them to plan the season (as well as individual games); recruit, organize, and train team members; effectively communicate goals, strategies, and tactics; procure resources; energize and inspire their teams toward winning; delegate accountability and authority for accomplishment of intermediate tasks and objectives to individual team members and sections (the process of empowerment); and reinforce the structure, society, disciplines, and habits of the team.

What a daunting array of skills! Strategist, tactician, organizer, trainer, motivator, communicator, delegator, psychologist, and disciplinarian—all rolled into one person!

POWER-THE CAPITAL OF LEADERSHIP

The degree to which a leader is able to influence the members of a team toward accomplishment of a goal is a measure of that leader's power. Leadership is, by its very nature, an exercise in the acquisition and use of power.

The term *power* carries, for some, negative or distasteful connotations. Yet, power is neither good nor evil. Like money, it is a commodity that is neutral. It may be used for proper or improper purposes. The choice of how it is used tells us all we need to know about the motives and goodness of leaders.

Wise leaders accumulate power in all of its forms and learn to select the proper form to address each problem that they encounter. Like a master carpenter, a wise leader has both a toolbox full of tools and the ability to employ each for its intended purpose.

CREDIBILITY-THE BASIS OF POWER

The basis of a leader's power and influence rests upon the leader's credibility. *Credibility* is the degree to which team members believe in their leader and that leader's ability and will to guide them in the right direction (whether that direction is popular or not). When a leader demonstrates characteristics, abilities, or behaviors that enhance his or her credibility in the eyes of team members, that leader's influence-the power to affect future actions of the team in the direction that the leader desires-also increases.

Conversely, when a leader's actions, behaviors, or demonstrated inabilities undermine his or her credibility, the leader's influence is discounted and power decreases. (See Figure 1-1, Credibility.)

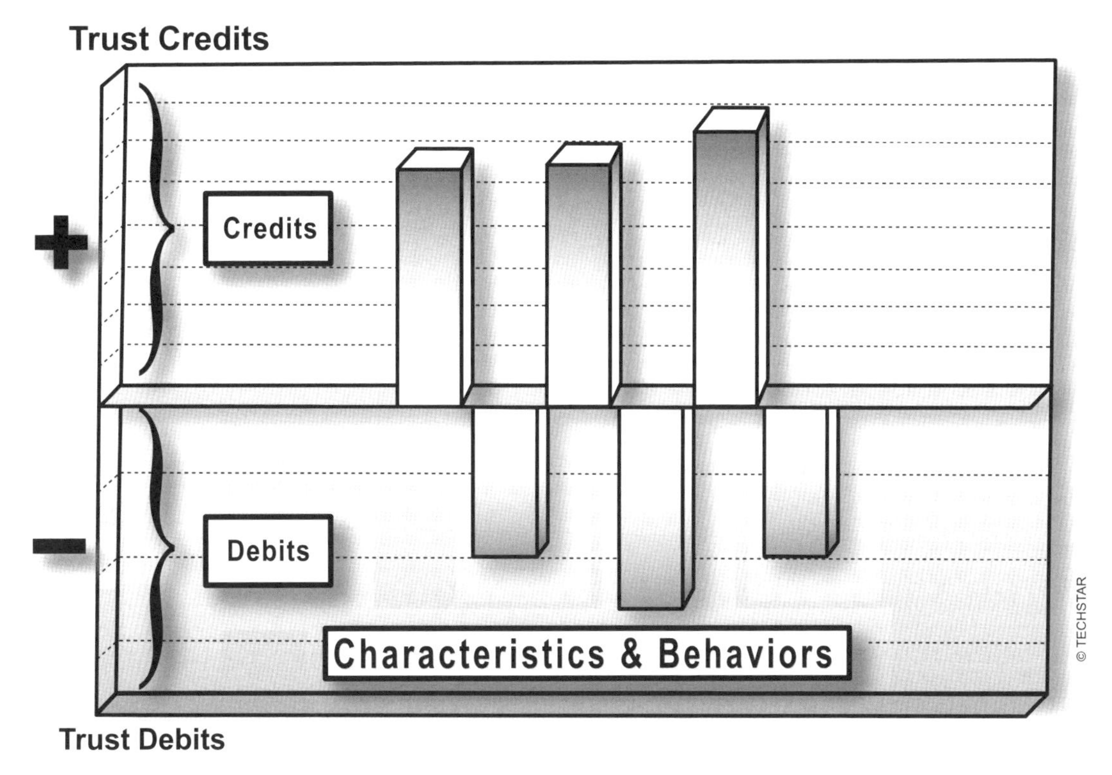

Figure 1-1 Credibility

In this elementary, yet complex relationship of leaders to team members, it seems obvious that whatever affects credibility also affects the power of a leader to influence the future actions of the team. Hence, credibility is the basis of a leader's power.

A MATTER OF TRUST

Lasting influence cannot be obtained without first acquiring the trust of the team. Ultimately, team members don't extend trust to leaders who mislead them through incompetence or dishonesty. So it's clear that honesty, competence, trust, and motivation are related.

Perhaps a short review of the two types of motivation would help us to see this relationship. Team members pursue the objectives of their leaders for one of two motives: *have-to* or *want-to*. (In the language of Frederick Herzberg, guru of motivational studies, *have-to* motivation is *extrinsic,* or from without. *Want-to* motivation is *intrinsic,* or from within.) Both are appropriate and necessary, depending upon the situation and the maturity of the team. *Have-to* motivation—coercion—is most useful in turning wayward individuals or organizations.

But *have-to* motivation falters in sustaining a team's forward motion since the actual objective becomes one of avoiding the consequences of non-compliance. Inevitably, *want-to* motivation is the path that leads to Olympic-level performance.

Trust is at the heart of *want-to* motivation. We don't long perform for leaders who lead us astray, either for want of technical competence or for lack of acumen in dealing with people. Leaders who are inept at directing the team's efforts, at best, discourage team members and, at worst, drive them into a cocoon of self-protectiveness, accompanied often with an attitude of sullenness or bitterness, two powerful performance poisons. In other words, we don't trust them.

EARNING TRUST-HOW LEADERS ACQUIRE INFLUENCE

How, then, is trust acquired? Demonstrated competence to lead is the answer—an earned worthiness to *call the shots*. In truth, the power that a leader exercises is usually a grant of confidence from team members to the team leader whereby individuals voluntarily harness (in concert with the leader's desires) their efforts to those of other members of the team for accomplishing an objective. They trust their leader to lead the team in the right direction for the right reasons.

Team members trust their leaders for two major reasons: demonstrated *technical* proficiency and demonstrated *people* proficiency (the ability to interact skillfully with others). Usually, neither alone is sufficient. Team members won't risk much on leaders who don't have technical competence, nor will they go the extra mile for people who don't deal squarely with them. Both issues are a matter of trust.

Note that both types of proficiency must be *demonstrated*. Team members are unwilling to trust in what they've never seen. Obviously, trust cannot be acquired without interaction.

LOSING TRUST-HOW LEADERS DISCREDIT THEMSELVES

So, how do leaders lose the trust of their team members? We're sure that you already know the answer to this question.

In our leadership seminars, we ask participants to envision the worst leader under whom they have ever served, whether parent, teacher, sports coach, military leader, church leader, government leader, or business leader.

The characteristics which most often surface in these discussions include dishonesty, technical incompetence, uninspiring demeanor, invisibility, selfishness, arrogance, failure to communicate, unfairness, inconsistency, disrespectfulness, indecisiveness, disloyalty, and cowardice.

These behaviors are *trust breakers*. Every time that a leader engages in such behaviors, team members become less trusting and less willing to do the will of that leader. Trust-eroding transactions reduce a leader's influence as team members subconsciously subtract from the bank account of trust that they have credited to their leader from previous interactions. In a sense, the leader's *trust bank account* (an account comprised of what psychologists used to call *idiosyncratic credits*) is depleted in a manner similar to the way an actual bank account is drawn down as checks are written. (See Figure 1-2, Earning and Losing Trust.)

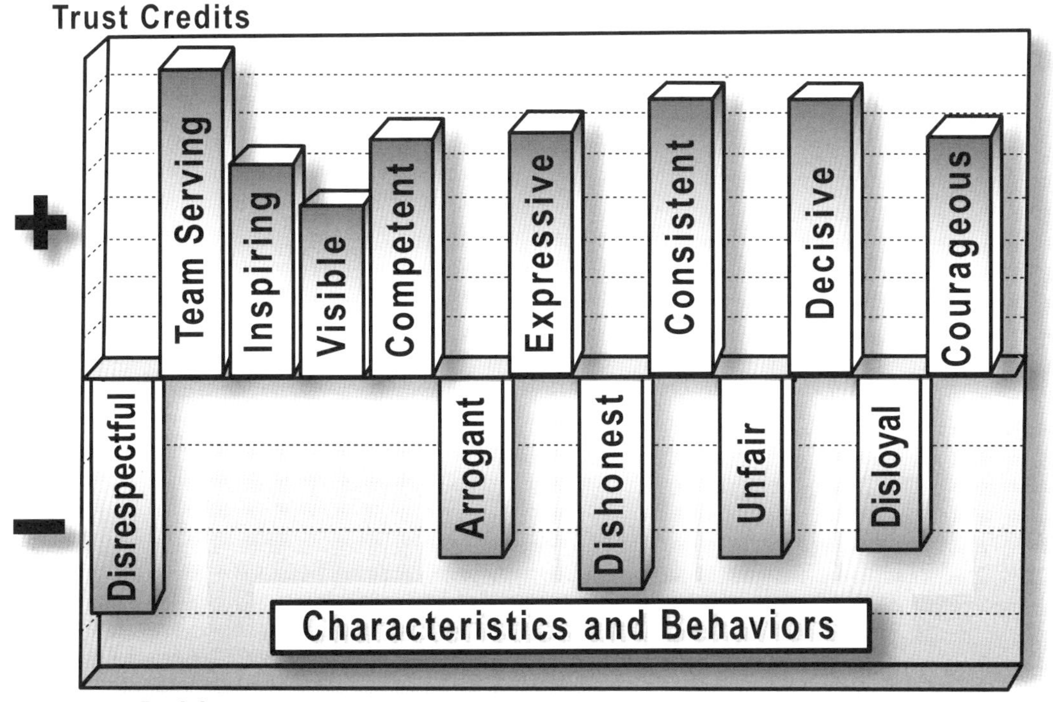

Figure 1-2 Earning and Losing Trust

TRUST BUILDING CHARACTERISTICS

Conversely, trust-building transactions (engendered by characteristics and behaviors that are the opposites of trust breakers) serve to fill the trust bank accounts of leaders. (See Figure 1-3, Total Trustworthiness.)

These behaviors and characteristics include:

- Honesty
- Technical Competence
- Inspiring Demeanor
- Visibility
- Team-Serving Attitude
- Humility
- Expressivity
- Fairness
- Consistency
- Respectfulness
- Decisiveness
- Loyalty
- Courage

DEPOSITS AND WITHDRAWALS ARE NOT EQUALLY VALUED

There is one subtle difference, however, between the trust-building and trust-breaking processes: *Team members seem to be less willing to credit leaders with trust when those leaders have shown themselves previously to be untrustworthy.* In other words, trust takes a long time to build but little time to lose. The more often a leader demonstrates untrustworthiness, the more team members tend to discount acts that should otherwise engender trust. Hence, the subsequent loss of influence may not be fully reversible through future acts.

If that conclusion is true, then it seems clear that leaders should strive to acquire and *maintain* credibility with team members! Please note, however, that at no point have we suggested that leaders should be "easy". Very few acts accord a leader more credibility than legitimate victories. Teams who are taught to grow and to win tend to be teams who revere their leaders. Much can be forgiven of a leader who leads a team to remarkable performance.

THE BOTTOM LINE

So, what's the bottom line? Leadership is a matter of trust. Leaders who engage in trust-breaking behaviors destroy their ability to lead.

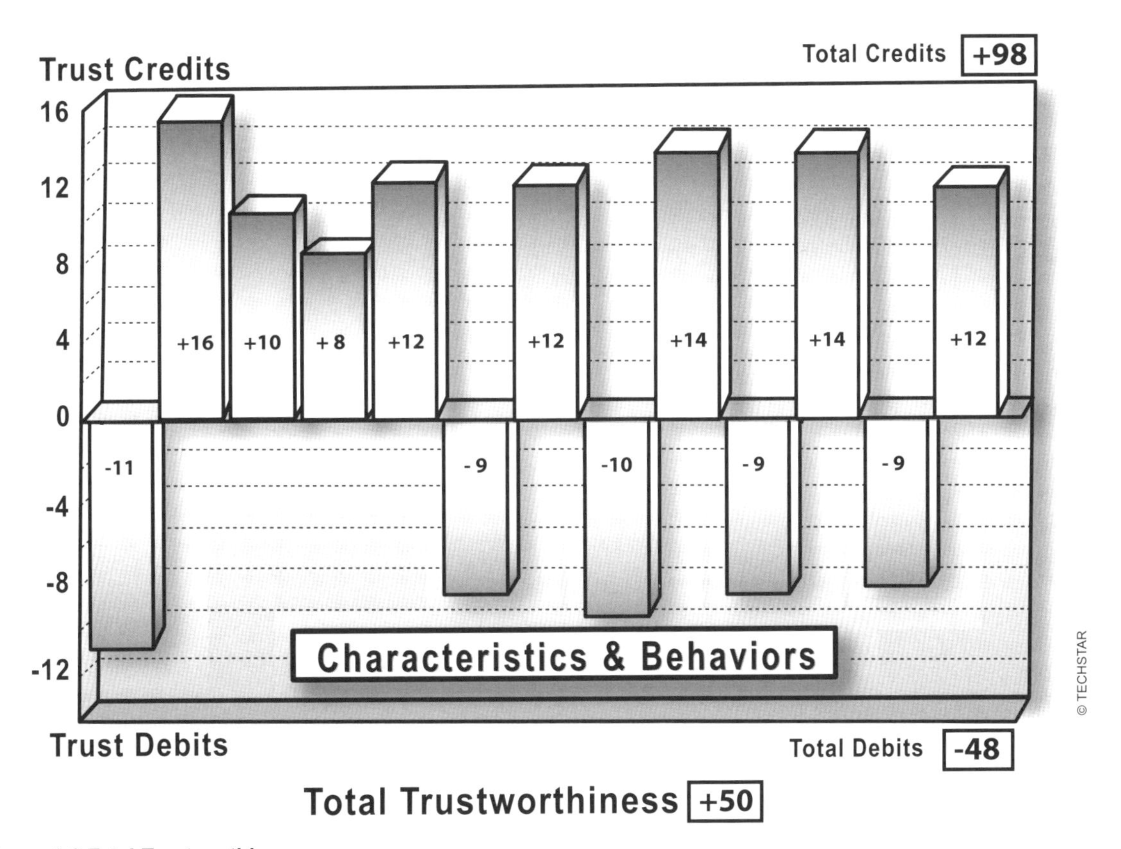

Figure 1-3 Total Trustworthiness

LEADING PRINCIPLE

The basis of a leader's power and influence rests upon the leader's credibility. When a leader demonstrates characteristics, abilities, or behaviors that enhance his or her credibility in the eyes of team members, that leader's influence also increases. Conversely, when a leader's actions, behaviors, or demonstrated inabilities undermine his or her credibility, the leader's influence and power are diminished. Team members lose trust in leaders who are inept at directing the team's efforts or who are not forthright in dealing with people.

Chapter 2

Character: A Foundation For Trust

"We don't willingly follow leaders who are of unsound character."

char•ac•ter (kăr'ək-tər) *n.* **1.** The combination of qualities or features that distinguish one person, group, or thing from another. **2.** A distinguishing feature or attribute… **4.** Moral or ethical strength. **5.** A description of a person's attributes, traits, or abilities.

THE trust extended by team members to a leader is founded predominantly upon the leader's character and competence. Without them, a leader has little upon which the team can stake its faith.

After the death of Robert E. Lee in October 1870, Benjamin H. Hill, a Representative and Senator from Georgia, extolled Lee's character with these words:

He was a foe without hate,
a friend without treachery,
a soldier without cruelty,
and a victim without murmuring.
He was a public officer without vices,
a private citizen without wrong,
a neighbor without reproach,
a Christian without hypocrisy,
and a man without guilt.
He was Caesar without his ambition,
Frederick without his tyranny,
Napoleon without his selfishness,
and Washington without his reward.

High praise for this former commander of the Army of Northern Virginia, one of the Great Captains. His technical competence was legendary (to the extent that many in the Grand Army of the Republic believed him invincible), but technical competence alone was insufficient. It was his character that inspired.

Charles Bracelen Flood, author of **Lee: The Last Years,** wrote:

> *They loved him as a commander has seldom been loved. His effect on his men was almost hypnotic. Before one battle Lee silently rode bareheaded along the lines of a regiment that was about to attack, paying tribute to the sacrifice they were going to make. It was a gesture so eloquent that one young soldier thought Lee had in fact made a speech, and charged the enemy sobbing and shouting, "Any man who will not fight after what Marse Robert said, is a damned coward!"*[1]

So what is character? Honesty? Reliability? Respectability? The way we treat others? Certainly it is all of those things, but it is also more. The test of character has often been defined as what we do when no one is watching. It is an internal compass-action commanded by conscience, built upon a moral foundation.

Character is a giant factor in the ability to lead. It inspires trust and confidence and sets a standard of behavior for other team members. The late and famed Tom Landry, former head coach of the Dallas Cowboys, wrote:

> *Give me a choice between an outstanding athlete with poor character and a lesser athlete of good character, and I'll choose the latter every time. The athlete with good character will often perform to his fullest potential and be a successful football player while the outstanding athlete with poor character will usually fail to play up to his potential and often won't even achieve average performance. Of course, when you can find an outstanding athlete with outstanding character you have the sort of rare player you can build a team around—people like a Bob Lilly, a Roger Staubach, or a Herschel Walker.*[2]

So it seems that great leaders must possess a combination of technical competence and high character. The technical competence comes, not merely from talent, but an attitude that places value on developing ability through hard work. Where, though, does character come from? Landry again:

> *I believe most of a person's character is developed as a child. It's the result of values learned from family and other significant people early in life—which is what makes our role as parents and the role of those who coach kids so important.*[3]

Character is not just in sports. Great team members and great coaches from every discipline—military, business, or sports—all sing the same refrain. In a 1990 interview with David Frost, Lady Margaret Thatcher, former Prime Minister of Great Britain, spoke of the need for character in serving her nation:

> *We were…taught very firmly to make up our own minds. Never just to follow the crowd because we didn't like to be different. I remember several times [asking], "Oh can't I do so and so or such and such. All my friends are doing it." Never do it because your friends are doing it. Make up your mind what you want to do and why you want to do it and then try to persuade others. It was quite a tough upbringing in that sense, but I have been eternally gratefully for it since. It IS right to make up your own mind. You never follow the crowd for the sake of it—because you are afraid to stand out and be different. I've had occasion to be very, very thankful for that during my period of office as Prime Minister and serving as a Member of Parliament.*[4]

To do the right thing. To make up your own mind. Never to follow the crowd for the sake of it. That attitude comes with a price, though. General Colin Powell, Chairman of the Joint Chiefs of Staff during the Gulf War, in an address to Sears executives, said, *"Being responsible sometimes means pissing people off."*[5]

Oren Harari (**The Leadership Secrets of Colin Powell**) explains:

> *Good leadership involves responsibility to the welfare of the group, which means that some people will get angry at your actions and decisions. It's inevitable—if you're honorable. Trying to get everyone to like you is a sign of mediocrity. You'll avoid the tough decisions, you'll avoid confronting the people who need to be confronted, and you'll avoid offering differential rewards based on differential performance because some people might get upset. Ironically, by procrastinating on the difficult choices, by trying not to get anyone mad, and by treating everyone equally "nicely" regardless of their contributions, you'll simply ensure that the only people you'll wind up angering are the most creative and productive people in the organization.*[6]

In other words, if popularity is your objective, you are unlikely to succeed as a leader.

THE BOTTOM LINE

So, what's the bottom line? Character is what makes you. It is a foundation upon which team members can rest their faith in a leader. Do you have character? Are you willing to do the right thing, even when it may lead to ridicule? Even if it's not popular? That's CHARACTER!!

LEADING PRINCIPLE	A leader's character is a giant factor in his or her ability to lead. High character inspires trust and confidence and sets a standard of behavior for other team members. A leader's character is tested by moral and ethical dilemmas, especially when the outcome of the decision might be hidden.

"Life can be likened to a grindstone.
Whether it grinds you down or polishes you
depends upon what you are made of."[7]

(John Maxwell)

Chapter 3

Adversity: The Forge Of Character

"We don't willingly follow leaders who can't handle difficulty!"

ad•ver•si•ty (ăd-vûr' sĭ-tē) *n.* **1.** A state of hardship or affliction; misfortune. **2.** A calamitous event.

IF character is such an indispensable asset to a leader, what must one do to acquire it? Unfortunately, it comes at great cost accompanied with much pain, dealt liberally by life itself.

At the end of the movie, **The Edge,** Anthony Hopkins' character, billionaire Charles Morse, said: "Everyone is put to the test, but it never comes in the form or at the point that we would prefer…"

Life is filled with adversity. It is inescapable, and none of us like it. Yet, no one (nor any team) can ever become strong without facing and overcoming adversity. Just as the labor of exercise builds muscle, it is through overcoming hardship and solving difficult problems that individual and team character are constructed.

Few of us ever choose hardship. It is not the nature of humans to seek difficulty; rather, we seek ease. Only as we are forced through the trials of life (and as we learn to subject ourselves to difficult training regimens administered by demanding, skilled coaches) do we learn that something lasting and valuable comes from conquering adversity.

J.C. Penney, founder of Penney's department stores, wrote: "I am grateful for all my problems. As each of them was overcome I became stronger and more able to meet those yet to come. I grew in all my difficulties."

Mr. Penney found strength and stamina for the future, not in the trials themselves, but in the struggle at overcoming them. Still, though, it's hard to be thankful for trials, especially while in their midst. They are often painful, frustrating, and, at the time, harmful. But dealing with them, learning from them, and then getting on with life is where the *muscle* of character is really built.

So why do some people know this and others don't, especially if it's such an important part of life? Is it an inherited trait, or is it learned? Probably it's a little of both. (The optimist may have a little easier time with it than the pessimist!) Usually though, the knowledge of the importance of attitude comes from a great coach—someone who invested his or her life in ours. Someone who cared enough to demand that we meet high standards and then patiently taught us how. That coach imparted an attitude, and attitude seems to be the difference between success and failure.

So, whether we whine and complain about our trials, or face them with the purpose of resolving them (and learning from them) tells everything about our character. Ultimately, it's a choice.

Tom Landry wrote:

> *As a leader you have to understand you will face adversity. In fact, it's so much a part of leadership that in the final evaluation, your reaction to adversity will determine your success or failure as a leader. A big part of the battle is a matter of attitude. As the philosopher William James said, "The greatest discovery of my generation is that human beings can alter their lives by altering their attitude of mind." You need to approach difficulties and adversities as a challenge to overcome rather than a problem to worry about. While you want to learn from past mistakes, you can't afford to look back. You have to be planning ahead. A leader can't afford to get too emotionally upset about the last mistake or the last play; you have to focus on what you will do differently next time.*[1]

So important is this choice—this attitude—that Landry sees in it the difference between successful leadership and failure.

It's not just Landry who knew this. Viktor Frankl, an Austrian psychiatrist who had the misfortune of being born Jewish in the world of Adolf Hitler, penned the classic book, **Man's Search for Meaning,** after surviving the horrors of the Nazi death camps. After his ordeal, he wrote:

> *The way in which a man accepts his fate and all the suffering it entails, the way in which he takes up his cross, gives him ample opportunity—even under the most difficult circumstances—to add a deeper meaning to his life. It may remain brave, dignified and unselfish. Or in the bitter fight for self-preservation he may forget his human dignity and become no more than an animal. Here lies the chance for a man either to make use of or to forgo the opportunities of attaining the moral values that a difficult situation may afford him. And this decides whether he is worthy of his sufferings or not.*[2]

He further wrote: *"We had to learn… that it did not really matter what we expected from life, but rather what life expected from us"*[3]—a mindset that he called "a fundamental change" in our attitude toward life.

If you study leadership long enough, you are going to find this "fundamental change" again and again in the lives of great leaders. It is an absolute. It is inescapable. It's what qualifies you to lead and encourage your team during hard times.

THE BOTTOM LINE

So, what's the bottom line? No one says it better than Scott Peck in **The Road Less Traveled:**

> *Life is difficult. This is a great truth, one of the greatest truths. It is a great truth because once we truly see this truth, we transcend it. Once we truly know that life is difficult—once we truly understand and accept it—then life is no longer difficult. Because once it is accepted, the fact that life is difficult no longer matters. Most do not fully see this truth that life is difficult. Instead they moan more or less incessantly, noisily or subtly, about the enormity of their burdens, and their difficulties as if life were generally easy, as if life should be easy. They voice their belief, noisily or subtly, that their difficulties represent a unique kind of affliction that should not be and that has somehow been especially visited upon them, or else upon their families, their tribe, their class, their nation, their race, or even their species, and not upon others. I know about this moaning because I have done my share. Life is a series of problems. Do we want to moan about them or solve them?* [4]

LEADING PRINCIPLE

No person (nor any team) can ever become strong without facing and overcoming adversity. Just as the labor of exercise builds muscle, it is through overcoming hardship and solving difficult problems that individual and team character are constructed. The attitude with which leaders face adversity is a critical indicator of whether those leaders will succeed.

Trust-Building Characteristics

- **Honesty:** The Cornerstone of Character
- **Technical Competence:** A Qualification for Coaching
- **Inspiration:** Breathing Life into the Team
- **Visibility:** A Leader I Can See
- **Unselfishness:** A Team-Serving Attitude
- **Humility:** Modesty of Spirit
- **Communication:** Painting Clear Pictures
- **Justness:** A Fair and Objective View
- **Consistency:** Walking the Talk
- **Respect:** A Two-Way Street
- **Decisiveness:** Someone Has to Make Choices
- **Loyalty:** Keeping Faith with the Team
- **Courage:** Commitment to Do Right

Trust is a matter of character, the qualities that comprise a leader's personality. Characteristics such as honesty, technical competence, visibility, and fairness inspire confidence in the minds of team members. They create a foundation upon which team members can stake their faith.

Chapter 4

HONESTY: THE CORNERSTONE OF CHARACTER

"We don't willingly follow leaders who lie to us!"

hon•est (ŏn'ĭst) *adj.* **1.** Marked by or displaying integrity; upright. **2.** Not deceptive or fraudulent; genuine. **3.** Equitable; fair. **4a.** Truthful; not false. **b.** Sincere; frank. **5a.** Of good repute; respectable. **b.** Without affectation; plain. **6.** Virtuous; chaste.

HONESTY is the cornerstone in the foundation of character. If a leader isn't honest team members are unlikely to trust the motives and reliability of the leader. Instead, they tend to act for their own self-protection, more than for team accomplishment.

Prominent in the definition of *honesty* are words such as truthfulness, genuineness, fairness, sincerity, and respectability. These are characteristics which form powerful bonds (common to all of our experiences) upon which team members will risk their reputations, their paychecks, and even their lives to support their leaders and the goals of their teams. They will literally bet the farm, and these characteristics have led to the coinage of phrases such as "She's as honest as the day is long," "You can bank on what he says," and "His word is as good as gold." These team members know that their leaders won't lie to them, won't paint a rosy picture when disaster is in the offing, won't confuse them, and won't lead them down the primrose path. They trust their leaders to give them a clear picture of the situation so that, as a team, they can meet their problems head on, fashioning reasonable solutions.

In contrast, team members who don't trust the words of their leaders are hesitant to act and seldom do so in concert. They spend much time trying to discern the motives of their leaders—time that could otherwise be spent in accomplishment. "How is he trying to trick us now?" becomes the question of the day.

Dishonesty is a team-breaker. It closes communication, sours attitudes, and discourages thoughtful risk-taking. Worst of all, it is a cancer that destroys those whom it inhabits. In his classic work **The Brothers Karamazov,** Fyodor Dostoevsky wrote:

> *A man who lies to himself, and believes his own lies, becomes unable to recognize truth, either in himself or in anyone else, and he ends up losing respect for himself and for others. When he has no respect for anyone, he can no longer love, and in order to divert himself, having no love in him, he yields to his impulses, indulges in the lowest forms of pleasure, and behaves in the end like an animal in satisfying his vices. And it all comes from lying—lying to others and to himself.*[1]

THE BOTTOM LINE

So, what's the bottom line? Don't lie to yourself or to other members of your team. Honesty is the cornerstone of character and forms the basis of trust. It takes a long time to build a reputation for honesty, but it only takes one lie to lose that reputation. Without honesty, no trust exists. Without trust, it is difficult to form the bonds of a cohesive team.

LEADING PRINCIPLE

Honesty is the quality of truthfulness of a leader. It is defamed by lies, broken promises, and duplicitous dealings with people. It begins with a conscience for serving others rather than self. (Is not dishonesty usually rooted in a selfish motive?) Honesty is demonstrated in each interaction with each person. It cannot be turned on or off at will. A leader with a reputation for dishonesty in the community is unlikely to obtain the respect and trust of a team at work.

"Excellent speech is not fitting for a fool;
Much less lying lips to a prince."
(Proverbs 17:7)

Chapter 5

Technical Competence: A Qualification For Coaching

"We don't willingly follow leaders who aren't technically competent!"

com•pe•tent (kŏm' pĭ-tənt) *adj.* **1.** Properly or sufficiently qualified; capable.

AN oft-pronounced dictum within management circles is that "a good manager can manage anything." Yet, it is difficult to place one's trust in a leader who does not possess the technical competence necessary to make sound technical decisions. How can one coach if one doesn't know how the game is played?

Clearly, leaders should seek and rely upon the knowledge of their team members, but leaders who are not soundly based in the technology of their professions work at a serious disadvantage. Not only are they limited in understanding, but they also do not inspire confidence in their team members. Players don't willingly follow coaches who don't understand the game.

In testimony before Congress following the Three Mile Island accident, Admiral Hyman Rickover, father of the U.S. Navy's nuclear power program, said:

> *One of the elements needed in solving a complex technical problem is to have the individuals who make the decisions trained in the technology involved. A concept widely accepted in some circles is that all you need is to get a college degree in management and then, regardless of the technical subject, you can apply your management techniques to run any program; including the Presidency, Congress, or the Vatican. This has become a tenet of our modern society, but it is as valid as the once widely held precept that the world is flat. Properly running a sophisticated technical program requires a fundamental understanding of and commitment to the technical aspects of the job and a willingness to pay infinite attention to the technical details. This can only be done by one who understands the details and their implications. The phrase "The devil is in the details" is especially true for*

> *technical work. If you ignore those details and attempt to rely on management techniques or gimmicks you will surely end up with a system that is unmanageable, and problems will be immensely more difficult to solve. At Naval Reactors, I take individuals who are good engineers and make them into managers. They do not manage by gimmicks but rather by knowledge, logic, common sense, and hard work.*[1]

Rickover believed that leaders without technical competence in their fields placed themselves and their teams at a distinct disadvantage.

Now, obviously, as a leader rises to higher ranks in an organization, minute technical detail becomes less important. Lee Iacocca, famous Chrysler CEO, would probably do well as the chief executive officer of a major airline, but, upon assuming the mantle of leadership, he would immediately surround himself with technically competent leaders and listen to their advice, tempering it with the wisdom of his years of experience in industry. His chief operating officer would assuredly have decades of technical as well as managerial experience.

As we have already stated, however, technical competence alone is not enough for sound leadership. People competence is at least as important. In **Success in War,** Patton wrote:

> *...[H]igh academic performance demands infinite, intimate knowledge of details, and the qualities requisite to such attainments often inhabit bodies lacking personality. Also, the striving for such knowledge often engenders the fallacious notion that capacity depends upon the power to acquire such details rather than upon the ability to apply them.*[2]

Finding people with balance between technical competence and people competence is extremely important in the development of expert leaders.

THE BOTTOM LINE

So, what's the bottom line? It's hard for one to be a soccer coach if one doesn't know how to play soccer!

LEADING PRINCIPLE Technical knowledge and skill are the bases upon which expertise power are built. Without them, leaders cannot fulfill the mentor role, cannot make wise decisions, and cannot effectively build and develop teams. In other words, it's impossible for incompetents to coach successfully.

"The mind of the prudent acquires knowledge,
and the ear of the wise seeks knowledge."

(Proverbs 18:15)

Chapter 6

INSPIRATION: BREATHING LIFE INTO THE TEAM

"We don't willingly follow leaders who leave us lifeless!"

in•spire (ĭn-spīr') *v.* **1.** To affect, guide, or arouse by divine influence. **2.** To fill with enlivening or exalting emotion **3a.** To stimulate to action; motivate. **b.** To affect or touch **4.** To draw forth; elicit or arouse…**5.** To be the cause or source of; bring about. **7.** *Archaic.* **a.** To breathe upon. **b.** To breathe life into…

INSPIRATION is an intangible, but vital character quality of a leader. Without it, a team is doomed to lifelessness.

Have you ever worked for someone whose enthusiasm was like that of Eeyore from the tales of Winnie the Pooh? Inspiring the team to victory in that Lee Marvin voice, "Well, I'm about as happy to be here as you are, so let's get this over with." It's pretty hard to get excited about the task and the team when the leader isn't excited (and isn't exciting).

During the Second World War, General Patton wrote to his wife, Beatrice, "I feel my claim to greatness hangs on an ability to inspire."[1] He told his commanders that, in his experience, "...nearly eighty per cent of [a leader's] mission is to arouse morale in his men."[2]

Clearly, Patton believed in the value of inspiration, but what does the term really mean? In its original form, the word *inspire* meant to breathe life into something. Isn't that what leaders are supposed to do? Breathe life into a group of talented people who otherwise would not be a team? In fact, such a "team" is just a body without life. To live, it needs a spirit.

The French named that spirit *esprit de corps*. The spirit of the body is the life of an organization that transcends every member of the team. That spirit is the source of *teamwork*—a synergy of organization in which the team is far greater than the sum of its individual team members.

Golda Meir, former Israeli Prime Minister, characterized the concept with these words:

> *All my country has is spirit. We don't have petroleum dollars. We don't have mines or great wealth in the ground. We don't have the support of a world-wide public opinion that looks favorably on us. All Israel has is the spirit of its people. And if the people lose their spirit, even the United States of America cannot save us.*

Such a spirit is only inspired—breathed into an organization—by its leaders.

THE BOTTOM LINE

So, what's the bottom line? If your organization is dead, guess whose job it is to INSPIRE it? Motivation begins with YOU!!

LEADING PRINCIPLE Pushes are sometimes necessary, especially in the training phases of teams. But, at the heart of leadership is the ability to inspire team members. It's what Coach Vince Lombardi meant when he said that real leaders get inside their people and motivate them.

"A joyful heart is good medicine,
But a broken spirit dries up the bones."

Proverbs (17:22)

Chapter 7

VISIBILITY: A LEADER I CAN SEE

"We don't willingly follow leaders who are not visible!"

vis•i•ble (vĭ' zə-bəl) *adj.* **1.** Possible to see; perceptible with the eye. **2a.** Obvious to the eye:... **b**. Being often in the public view; conspicuous **3.** Manifest; apparent... **4.** On hand; available...

HOW can you trust a leader whom you cannot see? Successful leaders know the importance of being seen, heard, and understood, and you cannot achieve that state by staying in the office.

When you think of Wendy's, who comes to mind? Dave Thomas! Though he's been gone from our midst for a few years, he was the symbol of Wendy's. Similarly, when you think of Chrysler, who comes to mind? Lee Iacocca! Yet, Mr. Iacocca hasn't led Chrysler (now Daimler-Chrysler) for over a decade. Or how about Southwest Airlines? Herb Kelleher! Yet, Herb recently retired. Microsoft? Bill Gates. Apple Computer? Steve Jobs. What is it about these leaders that attaches their images and their personalities so strongly to their companies that we still think of them as company leaders long after they have gone? They are visible, both to their team members and to the public.

People tend to learn and think in pictures. We have images streaming through our minds continuously. In fact, it's hard to understand a concept or even envision an object without first having seen it. This is especially true in leadership. If we don't have sound pictures of our leaders formed in both character and image, we may have difficulty devoting ourselves to serving the teams they lead.

Yet, it is incorrect to believe that visibility alone leads to the devotion of team members. The leaders named at the beginning of this chapter are legendary for their business acumen and commitment to their teams as well as their visibility;

but it's hard to become an icon without being seen. Ambrose Powell Hill, Robert E. Lee's III Corps Commander, wore a red shirt in battle so that he could be seen by his troops. Lee himself was a renowned image in the Army of Northern Virginia, visiting his soldiers and his officers with regularity. Ulysses S. Grant spent endless hours riding the lines, being seen by his men. Clara Barton, the "Angel of the Battlefield", was a welcome image among the soldiers of the Grand Army of the Potomac, crossing the pontoon bridge from Falmouth to Fredericksburg, VA, under fire with those she would soon treat for wounds. Patton used his presence and his image to motivate Second Corps and Third Army, and, in the arena of sports, just the sight of Phil Jackson (LA Lakers), Pat Summitt (Lady Vols), Joe Paterno (Nittany Lions), Bobby Knight (Texas Tech), or Mike Krzyzewski (Duke Blue Devils) along the sidelines of their respective fields of play inspires confidence in players and spectators alike. Even the sounds of their names arouse strong images and memories in the minds of those who know them personally or from afar.

There is a fine line, of course, between visibility and arrogance. If your motive is self-aggrandizement, then visibility is probably sought for the wrong reason; but if employed for the purpose of giving the team a tangible picture of a solid leader, then visibility becomes an irreplaceable asset.

THE BOTTOM LINE

So, what's the bottom line? Leaders need to be seen as well as heard!

LEADING PRINCIPLE Teams need the reassurance of a present and visible coach, a competent leader to whom they can look for guidance, support, and courage, especially during difficult times. It is that very visibility which allows a leader to lead by personal example, transmitting values through conduct, language, dress, emotional control, humor, and resoluteness.

Chapter 8

UNSELFISHNESS: A TEAM-SERVING ATTITUDE

"We don't willingly follow leaders who are self-serving instead of team-serving!"

self•ish (sĕl'-fish) *adj.* **1.** Concerned chiefly or only with oneself.

UNSELFISHNESS in a leader is the quality of putting the interests of the team first. Team members know that such a leader warrants their trust.

In the movie, **K-19: The Widowmaker**, Harrison Ford plays the role of a demanding submarine commander, Alexei Vostrikov. At the christening of K-19, he tells his crew: "Without me, you are nothing." Then, after his words sink in, he follows with: "Without you, I am nothing." Vostrikov's meaning was clear: just as teams serve their leaders, so do leaders serve their teams.

The focus of leadership is that the leader is a servant. Great leaders know that their job is to serve their teams—whether by demanding higher standards or through nurturing individual team members. The best leaders are not interested in self-aggrandizement. Rather, they recognize that *they* cannot succeed unless their teams succeed.

TEAM-SERVING OR SELF-SERVING?

If there is an acid test in separating good leaders from bad, it is probably the question, "Whom am I serving?" If the answer is "myself," I am likely far off track in my motive for leading.

Yet, leaders are no different than anyone else. They have self-interests. It's just that mature leaders have learned that serving the team first is a motivating gesture that returns great benefits. They have learned that the best way they can serve themselves is by serving the team.

CUSTOMER-ORIENTED

The leader's attitude of service extends, not only to the team, but to the customer as well. (See Figure 8-1, Whom Do I Serve?) It recognizes that, without the customer, the business team has no reason for existence. Tom Peters, former McKenzie associate and co-author of **In Search of Excellence**, explained:

> *The only way to get ahead in our view, regardless of what you are doing, is constant innovation and serving the customer right. And if that's true, it is crystal clear that it does not come from genius in the executive suite. It comes from respect for the dignity and the worth and the creative potential of every human being in the organization, pure and simple.*

The turn-around at Harley-Davidson in the 1990s is a strong testament to that attitude. Harley became a customer-oriented company, involving the rank and file team members of Harley in a campaign of constant improvement. Ownership and accountability became realities instead of platitudes.

Figure 8-1 Whom Do I Serve?

GIVING CREDIT TO OTHERS

How can a leader demonstrate unselfishness to the team? One sure way is through giving credit to the team when things go well.

In the movie, **Hoosiers**, following the success of the Hickory Huskers in the regional tournament, Coach Dale entered a gymnasium filled with reporters. One shouted, "Coach, how'd ya do it?" Coach Dale replied, "It wasn't me, it was the boys!"

In stark contrast to **Hoosiers** is the scene aboard the Destroyer/Mine Sweeper *Caine* in which the squadron leader passes a message of excellent performance to the *Caine*. Humphrey Bogart, in his extraordinary role as Lieutenant Commander Phillip Francis Queeg, from Herman Wouk's Pulitzer Prize winning novel, **The Caine Mutiny,** accepts the praise from the squadron leader, hangs up the radio handset, and keeps the information to himself as he continues to berate Ensign Willie Keith and Lieutenant Tom Kiefer for negligent performance of duty!

Success invariably comes from the excellent performance of the people in our organizations. The surest way to stimulate and sustain their motivation is the give them the credit. You, as well as they, will benefit. General Patton wrote to his commanders:

> *A General Officer who will invariably assume the responsibility for failure, whether he deserves it or not, and invariably give the credit for success to others, whether they deserve it or not, will achieve outstanding success.*[1]

In other words, when the team fails, leaders stand in the breach. When the team succeeds, leaders stand aside. Loyalty—the bond of trust—is the outgrowth.

President Dwight Eisenhower applied this principle in both military endeavors and in the arena of government:

> *In the hurley burly of a military campaign—or a political effort—loyal, effective subordinates are mandatory. To tie them to the leader with unbreakable bonds one rule must always be observed—take full responsibility, promptly, for everything that remotely resembles failure. Give extravagant and public praise to all subordinates for every success.*[2]

The General had learned that strong bonds of trust are built when leaders are quick to recognize the efforts of subordinates in a winning effort.

Great leaders from all walks of life have learned the value of giving credit. In **Be Quick—But Don't Hurry!**, Andrew Hill wrote of Coach John Wooden, yesteryear's renowned basketball mentor of the UCLA Bruins:

> *Coach realized that players, not coaches, win games, and he always deflected the press's attention away from himself and onto us. He was acutely aware of how sensitive the egos and psyches of the kids were, and he knew that they were the ones who needed to shoot, defend, and rebound. When postgame interviewers clamored for Coach to describe the turning point in a game, he never claimed that a change of defense or a great substitution turned the tide. Coach instinctively knew that by giving credit where it was due, his players would be happier and would win more games.*[3]

Of course, without the leadership of Coach Wooden, the team would never have reached greatness. (Remember what Buddy Wonkers said in the locker room before the state finals in the movie **Hoosiers**? "Let's win for Coach. He's the one who got us here.")

Great leaders grow beyond the need for constant adulation. They know that the chance to give credit to the team is a chance to strengthen the bonds of loyalty and trust within the team.

Yet, sometimes the team fails and leaders are tempted to avert blame, placing it on individual team members instead of shouldering the burden themselves. This is an alluring seduction that must be resisted. To succumb has a disastrous effect on team loyalty and trust. Andrew Hill wrote:

> *An important corollary to this is that the effective leader must always be willing to shoulder the blame for the shortcomings of his team. After all, every decision must ultimately be approved by the boss, so the boss must not look to deflect blame on those who made suggestions. Of course, that's why it is so much tougher to be the person in charge who has to decide, as opposed to an assistant whose role is to suggest… It takes a strong leader to accept the blame, but your organization will appreciate the strength it takes, and will reward it with loyalty.*[4]

THE BOTTOM LINE

So, what's the bottom line? The best way for you to serve yourself is to first serve your team.

LEADING PRINCIPLE

Unselfish, team-serving behavior is a difficult leadership characteristic to learn. Leadership is, by nature, an exercise in the use of power. It's easy to become intoxicated with power. (Remember Cambridge University historian Lord Acton's admonition? *Power corrupts; absolute power corrupts absolutely.)* Egotistical leadership, however, is a road to unwise decisions, poor judgment, and unclear thinking. There is no room for selfishness on any team. The behavior and attitude of a leader greatly influences team members to act in a similar manner. It is imperative, then, that leaders set the example for unselfish thinking and behavior. One way that leaders can demonstrate unselfish behavior is by giving credit to others (and taking the blame when things go wrong). It is a sure sign of confidence and maturity in the character of a leader. When you practice this principle, you will be rewarded with the loyalty of your team.

"The generous man will be prosperous,
And he who waters will himself be watered."
(Proverbs 11:25)

Chapter 9

HUMILITY: MODESTY OF SPIRIT

"We don't willingly follow leaders who seem overly impressed with their own importance!"

hum•ble (hŭm'bəl) *adj.* **1.** Marked by meekness or modesty in behavior, attitude, or spirit; not arrogant or prideful. **2.** Showing deferential or submissive respect…

ARROGANCE is a bitter trust-breaker. Most team members can sense its existence in the words and demeanor of a leader in a matter of minutes. All that the leader subsequently says or does is viewed through the lens of skepticism.

James Webb, former Secretary of the Navy during the Reagan Administration, and recently elected Senator from the State of Virginia, stated, "Humility before one's subordinates invites both loyalty and respect."[1] Since leadership is an exercise in the use of power, leaders sometimes fall prey to pride and arrogance. Yet, those qualities do not, as Mr. Webb indicates, invite either loyalty or respect, two qualities necessary for long term influence. In fact, prideful and arrogant leaders usually repel rather than attract subordinates.

Since power is a Lorelei, beckoning even experienced leaders to ruin, how does one maintain proper perspective? Perhaps the most important means is through recognizing that leadership is a trust—a sacred grant of influence with commensurate responsibility to use it wisely and graciously, not for personal gain, but for the betterment of the team. The motto "Serve to Lead" of the British Royal Military Academy at Sandhurst has that attitude in mind.

True leadership, then, is not self-serving but serves others. Great leadership comes only when leaders learn to suppress self-will and ego in deference to the team. In fact, the worthiness of a leader is often best determined by asking whom the leader serves first: himself or the team.

The concept of servant leadership is not a new one. King Solomon's prayer for wisdom, recorded in **II Chronicles** 1, is a clear illustration:

> *Give me now wisdom and knowledge, that I may go out and come in before this people; for who can rule this great people of Thine? And God said to Solomon, "Because you had this in mind, and did not ask for riches, wealth, or honor, or the life of those who hate you, nor have you even asked for long life, but you have asked for yourself wisdom and knowledge, that you may rule My people, over whom I have made you king, wisdom and knowledge have been granted to you. And I will give you riches and wealth and honor, such as none of the kings who were before you has possessed nor those who will come after you.* (**II Chronicles** 1:10-12)

In the same vein, Jesus admonished his disciples to beware of self-serving leadership:

> *...whoever wishes to become great among you shall be your servant, and whoever wishes to be first among you shall be your slave; just as the Son of Man did not come to be served, but to serve, and to give His life a ransom for many.* (**Matthew** 20: 26-28)

Yet, history is strewn with the wreckage of once great leaders who became enamored of their own positions. At the end of the movie, **Patton**, the General (played so eloquently by George C. Scott) reminds us that glory is not the reason for leading:

> *For over a thousand years Roman conquerors returning from the wars enjoyed the honor of a Triumph, a tumultuous parade. In the procession came trumpeters and musicians and strange animals from the conquered territories, together with carts laden with treasure and captured armaments. The conqueror rode in the triumphal chariot with the day's prisoners walking in chains before him. Sometimes his children, robed in white, stood with him in the chariot or rode the trace horses. A slave stood behind the conqueror, holding a golden crown and whispering in his ear a warning that all glory is fleeting.*

THE BOTTOM LINE

So, what's the bottom line? Arrogance is a trust killer. Humility invites respect.

LEADING PRINCIPLE

Arrogance is an unmistakable earmark of egotism. Arrogant leaders too often think of themselves before they think of the team. Humble leaders, on the other hand, focus on the team first. Because they are team-centered instead of self-centered, they can admit when they're wrong and laugh at themselves. Team members typically view them as human and compassionate, not as conceited and disdainful. As a result, they are usually respected leaders.

"... before honor comes humility."

(Proverbs 15:33)

Chapter 10

COMMUNICATION: PAINTING CLEAR PICTURES

"We don't willingly follow leaders who can't explain what they want us to do!"

com•mu•ni•cate (kə-myōō'-nĭ-ˌkāt') *v.* **1.a.** To convey information about; make known; impart. **b.** To reveal clearly; manifest:… **2.** To spread *(a disease, for example)* to others; transmit.

COMMUNICATION is the process of painting into the mind of another person the picture that is in one's own mind. It is a skill so essential to effective leadership that, without it, a leader is fatally impaired.

Leadership involves orchestrating the individual efforts of team members toward a common goal. Yet team members can't effectively pursue goals that they cannot see or do not understand. Subsequently, one of the leader's greatest challenges is to clarify final objectives, routes of approach, and intermediate objectives necessary to achieve the desired end. For that reason, communication is clearly fundamental to achievement of goals.

A goal-setting caution is in order here, however. Leaders sometimes over-control the goal-setting process, performing the task without team member input. For an immature or unskilled team, detailed control may be warranted; but, for a mature team, one of the most valuable methods of establishing goals that a team strongly supports is to let the team members determine the routes of approach and intermediate objectives. Patton said, "Never tell people **how** to do things. Tell them **what** to do and they will surprise you with their ingenuity."[1]

Team members who are actively involved in goal-setting usually acquire a clear picture of the intermediate objectives and the routes to achieve those goals since they themselves labored in their development. Patton's experience affirmed that concept:

> *Plans must be simple and flexible. Actually they only form a datum plane from which you build as necessity directs or opportunity offers. They should be made by the people who are going to execute them.*[2]

Verbal communication is, clearly, only a small part of the communication process. As the adage teaches, talk is cheap. What a leader does eventually overshadows what a leader says, because actions truly *do* speak louder than words. Leading by example, then, is an extraordinary means of communication. It is a process that creates clear pictures for subordinates who tend to emulate the behaviors of esteemed leaders.

Yet, nothing will destroy a team faster than a "Do as I say not as I do" leader. Trust, the glue of a team, dissolves rapidly in the face of dishonesty. Ridicule and hatred eventually take the place of trust, and, in the worst cases, open scorn prevails. At that point, the "team" has probably become dysfunctional individual parts.

Nowhere in film has this pattern been better portrayed than in **The Caine Mutiny.** Humphrey Bogart portrays just such a leader in the character of Queeg. His duplicitous behavior leads ultimately to the unraveling of his team. Watching the process arouses strong emotions in most of us, probably because we have experienced the injustice of dishonesty in a leader. The lesson is clear:

DON'T TELL YOUR PEOPLE TO DO ONE THING
WHILE YOU DO ANOTHER!!

The techniques for establishing and maintaining effective communication in a team are no different than for a family. Interchanges must be respectful, honest, clear, and tactful where possible. Team members and team leaders must attempt to state their points plainly without doing damage unnecessarily.

Yet, a climate of open communication does not mean that an organization is free of friction. (Even though an engine is properly lubricated, it still generates heat; without enough clean oil, the engine will eventually seize. So it is with organizations.) Friction is inevitable if honesty and improvement are valued. Movement doesn't occur without resistance in this imperfect world.

It is precisely because of this climate of openness and honesty that communication is sometimes abrasive. In other words, it hurts! Team members must recognize that failing to communicate difficult points—points that might hurt someone's feelings—does a disservice to the team. So they need to muster up the courage necessary to raise tough issues. Here is a communications key to creating a professional team: *Team members must learn to convey tough issues in a manner conducive to improvement, not self-aggrandizement.*

If the communication climate is so important, then how is it established? The responsibility for creating an environment that supports open interchange rests predominantly with the principal leader. Leaders set the tone. If shooting the messenger is the habit, communication will quickly close.

The method of delivering a message is at least as important as the message content. That's a critical lesson for leaders—so critical, in fact, that we will revisit the subject in another section on giving and receiving criticism.

THE BOTTOM LINE

So, what's the bottom line? Paint clear, consistent pictures for your team in word and in deed.

LEADING PRINCIPLE

Teamwork is impossible without effective communication. It is through communication that teammates learn values, share ideas, set goals, and obtain the perspective for resolving problems. It is essential, then, that leaders be communicative, but a leader does not have to be extroverted to communicate effectively. In fact, quiet, listening leaders are better for some organizations and some situations. The key is not how loudly the message is delivered, but rather its clarity and persuasiveness. Remember, Abraham Lincoln, though friendly, was not extroverted, yet by painting into the minds of his listeners the pictures that were in his own mind, he was one of the most effective communicators of the 19th Century.

"Without consultation, plans are frustrated,
But with many counselors they succeed."

(Proverbs 15:22)

Chapter 11

Justness: A Fair And Objective View

"We don't willingly follow leaders who aren't fair!"

just (jŭst) *adj.* **1.** Honorable and fair in one's dealings and actions... **2.** Consistent with what is morally right; righteous: *a just cause.* **3.** Properly due or merited. **4.** *Law* Valid within the law; lawful. **5.** Suitable or proper in nature; fitting. **6.** Based on fact or sound reason; well-founded: *a just appraisal...*

WE are all afflicted by biases. We see things through filters which have been established through years of education and experience, and from perspectives derived from our personalities, yet leaders are expected to view circumstances and to interact with people in a fair and objective manner. It's a difficult task, especially if we don't like the person with whom we are interacting.

Since leaders often have within their power the means to treat someone unjustly (let's say for the sake of vengeance) without personal consequence, it takes a leader of high character to forego the opportunity, one who views the circumstance from the perspective of what is good for the team instead of what is personally satisfying. (Remember that the leader must be team-serving in preference to being self-serving.)

We are *not* saying here that past actions shouldn't affect a team member's present treatment. Team members who have not done their jobs and have not been team players should not be accorded the same treatment and benefits as ones who have contributed greatly to the team. In fact, it would be *unjust* to do so. For, as in the American jurisprudence system, past performance usually affects current treatment under the law, so it should be in a business organization. What we are saying is that just behavior means using one's power and position reasonably and fairly considering the circumstances. Team members may not like a leader who enforces standards justly, but they usually recognize if the treatment is fair.

Included in the concept of justice are the extremes of discipline—reward and punishment. When used wisely, these tools reinforce the value of justice within a team, but when punishment or reward is not warranted, a sense of injustice grows within the team. Team members know, for the most part, when punishment is warranted for purposeful violations, even if they grumble about it. Similarly, they know when a team member's performance is so noteworthy as to warrant reward.

Much of a leader's reputation is built upon the fair (or unfair) use of power. Just treatment of team members puts credits in a leader's trust bank. Unjust treatment depletes the account rapidly.

THE BOTTOM LINE

So, what's the bottom line? Leaders who are fair may not always be liked, but, usually they will be respected.

LEADING PRINCIPLE Prejudicial behavior (making judgments in the absence of fact), unfair dealings with peers and subordinates, and unreasonable demands are all destructive behaviors that destroy the credibility and effectiveness of leaders. Conversely, objectivity, fairness, and circumspect dealings create a climate of respect and openness, the climate in which complex problems are more likely to be solved.

*"A false balance is an abomination to the LORD,
But a just weight is his delight."*

(Proverbs 11:1)

Chapter 12

Consistency: Walking The Talk

"We don't willingly follow leaders who say one thing and do another!"

con•sis•ten•cy (kən-sĭs'tən-sē) *n.* **1a.** Agreement or logical coherence among things or parts. **b.** Correspondence among related aspects; compatibility. **2.** Reliability or uniformity of successive results or events.

in•teg•ri•ty (ĭn-tĕg'rĭ-tē) *n.* **1.** Steadfast adherence to a strict ethical code. **2.** The state of being unimpaired; soundness. **3.** The quality or condition of being whole or undivided; completeness.

VERY little is as destructive to trust and to a team as a leader who says one thing and does another. Inconsistent behaviors and standards leave a bitter taste in the mouths of team members. Leaders who demand standards from others that they, themselves, cannot or will not meet are said to lack *integrity*, a concept closely aligned with that of honesty.

However, we should not confuse same standards with same treatment. Here is one of the great paradoxes of leadership: *Though the standards for team members should be the same, the methods necessary to lead them toward achievement of those standards must often be different!* How many of you have children born to the same parents and raised in the same home, but who have diametrically different personalities? You have probably learned that the training that works for one child doesn't necessarily work for the other. Rather, to be a successful parent, you have learned that you must know your child and provide the discipline that is best for him or her.

The same dilemma applies for leaders in business organizations, military units, or sporting teams. In **Paterno: By the Book,** Coach Joe Paterno put it this way:

> *Eventually, through trial and error, I found out there are different ways to handle different people. So I began to be a coach. I remember saying to Rip*

> [Rip Engle, one of Joe's mentors at Brown University] *one day, "How can that kid have such a different outlook on football than that other kid from the same high school, same football program? How can he be so gung ho to practice while that other kid can't get himself out of first gear" Rip said, "Joe, the longer you're in this business, the more you're going to realize that everybody's different." I heard him say that, and it entered my head, but I still had trouble buying it until I had my own family. Then I saw for myself: same home, same parents, and look how different my own kids are.*[1]

Coach Paterno reminds us that we must be consistent with our teams and, yet, inconsistent in the way we treat each member of the team. On first examination, that may seem unfair; but in the light of experience, each of us knows that Coach Paterno's observations are wise. Every team member is at a different level of maturity, has a different disposition, and so possesses a different personality. As a result, each team member needs different handling.

About now, it should be dawning on us that we can't actually lead a team successfully without knowing the members of the team, and we never can know the team members without interacting with them. One of the great tasks of leaders is to interact on a daily basis with some segment of the team, whether a single member or a small contingent. It is through these interactions that we learn the nature of our teams, the state of team thinking and morale, and the obstacles that the team sees as barriers to success.

One other thought about the consistency of leaders: Leaders who are unable to control their emotions do not serve their teams well. Decisions made from a platform of emotional instability are often unwise. Further, leaders who routinely lose their tempers send the message to team members that lack of emotional control is an acceptable trait. On the other hand, emotional control is often displayed by the ability of a leader to remain calm in crisis.

THE BOTTOM LINE

So, what's the bottom line? Leaders must be consistent in standards while, at the same time, giving each player the encouragement he or she needs to improve performance.

LEADING PRINCIPLE The characteristics of integrity and consistency tell team members that their leader is "whole or undivided" in thinking and that they can expect "logical coherence" in behavior and standards. Such leaders don't just talk standards and practices. They live them as well. Such behavior tends to inspire trust and commitment, two important ingredients in the concoction of a team.

"The integrity of the upright will guide them."

(Proverbs 11:3)

Chapter 13

RESPECT: A TWO-WAY STREET

"We don't willingly follow leaders who treat us disrespectfully!"

re•spect (rĭ-spĕkt') *n.*. **1.** A feeling of appreciative, often deferential regard; esteem. **2.** The state of being regarded with honor or esteem. **3.** Willingness to show consideration or appreciation.

THERE are two kinds of respect. One is related to an office held and the other is based upon behavior. Have you ever heard someone say, "Well, I may have to respect the position, but I don't have to respect the person?" The first type of respect is an acknowledgment of authority vested in an office. The second refers to personal respect garnered by one who occupies the position. For example, the office of President of the United States commands a large degree of respect, but the person occupying the office may behave in a manner that engenders disrespect. We should render respect to the President, no matter whom the President is, yet the second type of respect—personal respect—must be earned.

As with loyalty and trust, both types of respect tend to be two-way streets. We should neither anticipate respect if we have not first accorded it, nor should we believe that we will be regarded with personal respect if we have not earned it.

Respect should not be confused with popularity. A leader does not have to be popular to be respected. You have probably learned that principle by raising children. You know that you can reprimand or even punish a child and be very unpopular, at least for some time, but if you have been fair, your child probably knows it and likely regards you with grudging respect—even during your unpopular period!

The same concept applies as we lead our teams. As we noted in the section on justice and fairness, team members usually know when punishment or reward is warranted. Neither they nor we like the reprimand or punishment part, but if fairly rendered, the leader is usually respected.

THE BOTTOM LINE

So, what's the bottom line? Respect is a two-way street. If you want it, you must give it.

LEADING PRINCIPLE	Though team members are (or, at least, should be) bound to respect a leader's *position*, they are *not* bound to respect the leader. Personal respect is earned through fair and respectful dealings with team members, proof of professional competence, and professional demeanor.

Chapter 14

Decisiveness: Someone Has To Make Choices

"We don't willingly follow leaders who can't make up their minds!"

de•ci•sive (dĭ-sī'-sĭv) *adj.* **1.** Having the power to decide; conclusive. **2.** Characterized by decision and firmness; resolute. **3.** Beyond doubt; unmistakable…

HAVE you ever worked for a leader who had the characteristics of a windsock—controlled by the prevailing wind direction and filled to the extent that wind velocity dictated? That's an unfortunate quality for a leader, because leaders often have to lead their people against the "corporate winds." Such is the nature of change and progress, the stock and trade of leaders.

Teams are complex problem-solving machines, gifted with diverse viewpoints and skills. In the process of solving problems, a team is usually confronted with choices at every bend in the complex problem-solving road. Every potential path is characterized by advantages and disadvantages, some of which accrue in the long term and some in the short. Someone has to choose the direction at each bend in the road after weighing those advantages and disadvantages.

On good teams, there are capable and responsible leaders at every level who should be making evaluations and decisions on the scene so the primary leader isn't overwhelmed with problem solving. Usually, team members appreciate team leaders and section leaders who are capable and willing to make choices at critical junctures, choices which allow complex problem-solving to continue. The decisiveness of a leader (if predicated upon sound judgment) builds confidence and encourages informed risk-taking.

On the other hand, leaders whose words and actions indicate that they don't know where they're going (or why they're going there) don't inspire confidence and trust. Instead, a team led by one who is excessively fearful of making an unpopular or wrong choice may find that a window of opportunity has closed while the team awaited direction. They may be "overcome by events." That's a discouraging feeling, one that detracts substantially from a leader's trust bank.

Leaders' decisions are not always right. Sometimes, the available data is insufficient or so unclear in meaning that choices are poorly supported. Yet, direction may be immediately necessary. So, in retrospect, leaders sometimes find themselves on the wrong side of a decision. It happens to each of us, but that's why there are leaders. Someone must decide. Fortunately, our mistakes are usually evaluated in the light of a track record rather than a single instance.

One final thought: *Fast decision-making is not always a desirable quality.* As we have already seen, decisiveness needs to be tempered with good judgment. Unfortunately, good judgment usually comes from experience, and experience usually comes from bad judgment!

THE BOTTOM LINE

So, what's the bottom line? Define the problem, seek input, and make a choice. As General Patton admonished, "The best is the enemy of the good."[1]

LEADING PRINCIPLE	Decisiveness describes the ability of a leader to make decisions in a timely manner based upon the information that is reasonably available. Decisiveness should not be confused with good judgment. Fast decisions are not necessarily good decisions. Similarly, delayed decisions can often be disastrous. Good judgment must always temper decisiveness.

"The best is the enemy of the good."
(General George S. Patton Jr.)

Chapter 15

Loyalty: Keeping Faith With The Team

"We don't willingly follow leaders who don't support us!"

loy•al (loi'əl) *adj.* **1.** Steadfast in allegiance to one's homeland, government, or sovereign. **2.** Faithful to a person, ideal, custom, or duty.

LOYALTY is the quality of faithfulness to a person, an organization, a country, or a cause. It is a demonstration of commitment and support in the face of difficulty.

In the movie **Hoosiers**, when Coach Dale introduced his team to the school assembly, a chant arose for Jimmy Chitwood, the best of the players who had chosen not to play on the team. Coach Dale strode to the microphone and said:

> *I was hoping you would support who we are, not who we are not. These six individuals have made a choice to work, a choice to sacrifice and put themselves on the line twenty-three nights in the next four months to represent you, this high school. That kind of commitment and effort deserves and demands your respect. This is your team.*

Those words were not popular with the crowd. Coach Dale was taking a risk in uttering them, but he needed to teach two lessons: one to the school and one to his team. To the school was the lesson of respect for sacrifice and commitment. To his team was the lesson that he would support them in the face of adversity. He demonstrated his allegiance to them, something that is hard to forget.

Loyalty is what carries a team through hard times. When things get rough, it's tempting to abandon the team or the team leader, but when team members and leaders have sacrificed for one another, an attachment of loyalty is born. We feel responsible *for* and *to* each other. Without it, teams fall apart during times of difficulty and stress.

Loyalty cannot be built without honesty and just dealings. It is an outgrowth of trust. Leaders who lie to their teams or treat them with disrespect should not expect loyalty in return.

Where, then, does loyalty begin? General Patton believed that the growth of loyalty begins at the top, with the leaders:

> *There is a great deal of talk about loyalty from the bottom to the top. Loyalty from the top down is even more necessary and much less prevalent.*[1]

Patton had learned that loyalty isn't something that leaders can demand or create when necessary. It must be cultivated and nurtured for the future.

THE BOTTOM LINE

So, what's the bottom line? Your team members may not always choose or perform correctly, but if they are operating in good faith, they deserve your support.

LEADING PRINCIPLE

Loyalty is the quality of faithfulness to a person, an organization, a country, or a cause. Loyalty, as all other leadership characteristics, is contagious. Conversely, disloyalty will destroy a fundamentally good organization rapidly. Loyalty holds a team together when difficulties try to tear it apart. It is a product of trust, born of forthright, just dealings with one another. Loyalty is a two-way street. If I want loyalty *from* my team, I must demonstrate loyalty *to* my team.

"A friend loves at all times,
And a brother is born for adversity."

(Proverbs 17:17)

Chapter 16

Courage: Commitment To Do Right

"We don't willingly follow leaders who won't take a stand!"

cour•age (kûr'-ĭj) *n.* The state or quality of mind or spirit that enables one to face danger, fear, or vicissitudes with self-possession, and resolution; bravery.

COURAGE is not the absence of fear but the determination and commitment to face fearful situations. In **War as I Knew It**, Patton wrote:

> *If we take the generally accepted definition of bravery as a quality which knows not fear, I have never seen a brave man. All men are frightened. The more intelligent they are, the more they are frightened. The courageous man is the man who forces himself, in spite of his fear, to carry on. Discipline, pride, self-respect, self-confidence, and the love of glory are attributes which will make a man courageous even when he is afraid.*[1]

Of course, Patton was writing about the fear and physical courage of those facing the dangers of combat. In the modern business world, we are seldom called upon to demonstrate physical courage. Instead, business men and women are challenged with making choices in environments fraught with financial, career, and ethical risk, decisions that may dramatically affect their own lives and the lives of their team members. They are confronted with the need for *moral courage*.

Moral courage describes the propensity of a leader to make decisions based upon principle rather than upon special interest pressures or personal biases. In stressful times, all of us are tempted to take the easy road. Our motive may be to avoid the ridicule of peers, to achieve financial gain for ourselves or our companies, or to polish our images. An old American adage warns, "Where principle is involved, be deaf to expediency."

It takes moral courage to walk the high road. West Point's Cadet Prayer admonishes cadets always to "choose the harder right instead of the easier wrong—never to be content with a half-truth when the whole can be won." Yet, do most of us identify straight-forward truth-telling as an act of courage? The recent corporate and financial scandals of several large American companies cast a discouraging pall on that concept. It's difficult to feel compassion for corporate leaders as they tearfully express their regrets and claims of innocent intent when the facts of their trials show personal greed that led to the bilking of investors of billions of dollars. Such cases cause us to ask how those leaders (and their boards) could have achieved elevated levels of leadership without understanding how courage and truth-telling are related.

THE BOTTOM LINE

So, what's the bottom line? Fear is not a sign of weakness. (If you don't experience fear, perhaps you are unaware of the risk!) Moreover, recklessness is not courage. Instead, courage is shown by resoluteness and commitment.

LEADING PRINCIPLE

Courage is the quality of character which allows one to face danger, not without fear, but with the resoluteness and confidence that comes from doing what is right. It may be displayed physically or morally. Physical courage is not often required in the modern business world, but *moral* courage is. Moral courage describes the propensity of a leader to make decisions based upon principle rather than upon special interest pressures or personal biases (even if the leader stands to lose personally by such action). A leader lacking moral courage is likely to act unethically, since doing the right thing is often difficult.

Trust-Building Skills

- Understanding Your Role
- Knowing Yourself
- Motivating the Team
- Balancing People and Production
- Caring for the Team
- Using Power and Influence
- Navigating the Corporate Terrain
- Disciplining the Team
- Encouraging Criticism

The role of leader is multi-faceted, requiring the skills of strategist, tactician, teacher, motivator, communicator, psychologist, and disciplinarian. To fulfill those roles, leaders must know themselves, their teams, their tools, and their chosen disciplines. As leaders competently discharge those responsibilities, team members extend trust to their leaders and acquire confidence in their teams.

Chapter 17

Understanding Your Role

"We don't willingly follow leaders who don't know their purpose!"

lead (lēd) *v.* **led** (lĕd), **lead•ing, leads**—*tr.* **1**. To show the way to by going in advance. **2.** To guide or direct in a course: *lead a horse by the halter*. **4**. To guide the behavior or opinion of: induce: *led us to believe otherwise*. **5a**. To direct the performance or activities of. **b.** To inspire the conduct of: *led the nation*.

WHAT do leaders do? What functions do they fulfill in the structure of a team? Tommy Lasorda, long associated with Dodger's baseball, was asked what managers do. He replied that he didn't hit the ball anymore, he didn't field the ball anymore, and he didn't throw the ball anymore. His job, he said, was to get his players to play more for the name on the front of their jerseys than the one on the back!

Leadership is both simple and complex. Leaders wear many hats, but when you distill the leader's role to its essence, it's hard to describe it any better than did Coach Lasorda. Figure 17-1, Functions of a Leader, is a graphical view of some of the roles that leaders fulfill.

VISIONARY

It is difficult (and dangerous) to follow someone who doesn't know where he's going. In the book of **Matthew**, Jesus admonished:

> *...they are blind guides of the blind. And if a blind man guides a blind man, both will fall into a pit.*

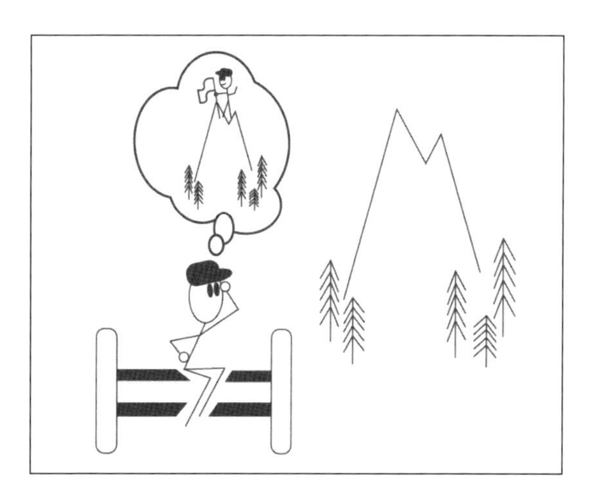

Vision, then, is a critical function of leadership. Good leaders need to have a clear view of the road ahead and a good understanding of where that road leads, or they cannot effectively guide the team. Bill Parcells, perennial NFL head coach, wrote in **Finding a Way to Win**:

> *When leaders have a vision, they can picture the desired result of a project before they begin...*[1]

By picturing the desired result, a good coach is able to communicate the vision to team members and to set a course to achieve the desired objective.

Painting clear pictures has another important benefit: when the pathway is clear and the objective in sight, skilled team members usually don't need to wait for the leader's direction. Instead, with clear pictures, team members are able to initiate action immediately. As a result, the team's actions become fluid and harmonious, and that's what creates synergy.

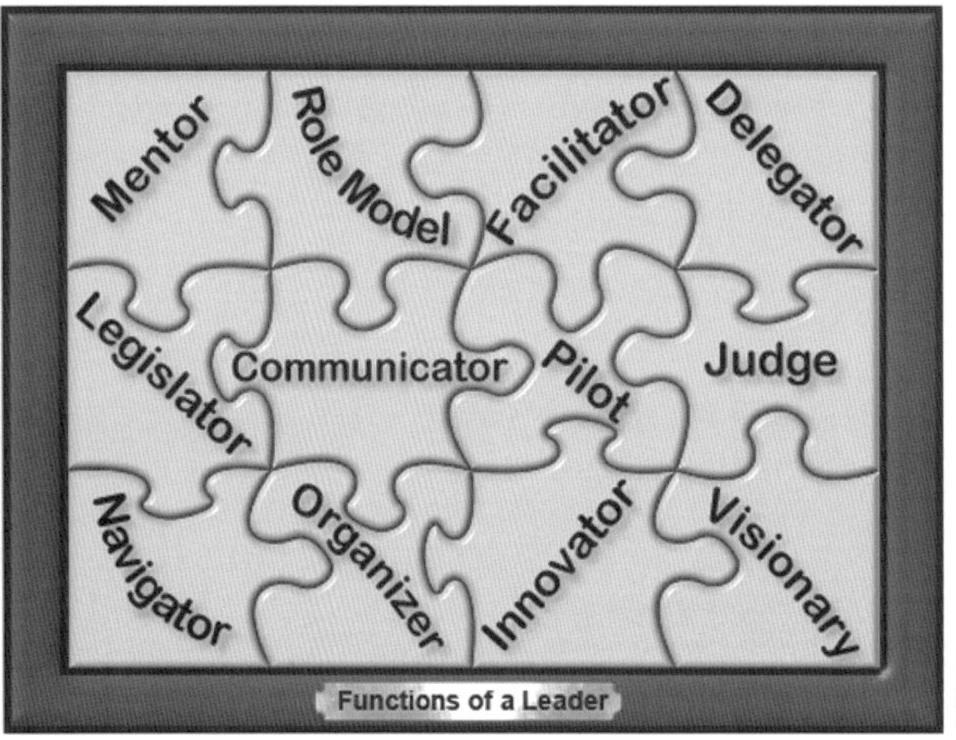

Figure 17-1 Functions of a Leader

COMMUNICATOR

Creating clear images of objectives, pathways, intermediate goals, and the techniques for achieving them is central to effective leadership. Consequently, the skill of communicating, perhaps more than any other function, is essential to leading. Historical studies of great leaders never fail to emphasize their communication skills to their subjects. During the Second World War, Sir Winston Churchill rallied the citizens of the British Empire in a way never before seen by the world. President Lincoln's words of commitment on the hallowed grounds of Gettysburg and during his second inauguration are legendary. Dr. Martin Luther King's "I Have a Dream" oration became the touchstone for the American Civil Rights movement, and the lines drawn by Lady Margaret Thatcher and President Ronald Reagan during the Cold War are renowned for their clarity.

You don't need to be as eloquent as those just named to be effective. Clarity is the key. Through descriptive words, attitudes, and actions, leaders can successfully impart the images and demonstrate the behaviors necessary for team accomplishment.

ROLE MODEL

No more powerful form of communication exists, either for good or for bad, than the example of a leader. Good ones inspire trust, commitment, and loyalty. Bad ones tear teams apart. Actions really do speak louder than words, and nothing destroys a team faster than a "Do as I say, not as I do" leader.

Team members need someone that they can look up to—a role model—someone to set the example. Senator James Webb, former Secretary of the Navy and noted author, remarked:

A true leader must set the example. You cannot ask of your subordinates that which you do not demand of yourself. And one who does not set the example will never be respected.[2]

Senator Webb speaks with some experience, having successfully commanded a platoon of Marines in combat during the Vietnam conflict. His no-nonsense leadership approach was heartily cheered by the Annapolis midshipmen (and sometimes abhorred by top Navy brass)!

As a role model, the leader fulfills the functions of motivator, source of inspiration, standard setter, and standard bearer. By exhibiting desirable attributes, attitudes, and skills, a good leader leads *by example*, communicating the characteristics and behaviors expected of the team.

MENTOR

You can't be a good role model without contact, not just with team members, but with the upcoming generation of leaders. If you research the backgrounds of great leaders, you almost always find other great leaders. Patton learned his trade as aide to General John "Blackjack" Pershing prior to the First World War. Pershing later was appointed to create and command the American Expeditionary Force whose service during the First World War turned the tide of events in Europe. General Dwight Eisenhower learned at the foot of General Douglas MacArthur, whose service in three of our nation's wars is legendary. The same phenomenon is apparent in the study of the lineage of great sports coaches. You need only trace the names of professional football coaches who got their starts under Bill Walsh of the San Francisco '49ers or Tom Landry of the Dallas Cowboys. Leaders learn habits, whether good or bad, from other leaders.

The lineage of leaders is no less apparent in business. Robert Townsend, author of **Further Up the Organization,** wrote:

> *When I became head of Avis I was assured that no one at headquarters was any good, and that my first job was to start recruiting a whole new team. Three years later, Hal Geneen, the president of ITT (which had just acquired Avis), after meeting everybody and listening to them in action for a day, said, "I've never seen such depth of management; why, I've already spotted three chief executive officers." You guessed it. Same people. I'd brought in only two new people, a lawyer and an accountant.*[3]

Townsend's experience was not a coincidence. His talented people were taking their cues from the boss, learning in his presence, and emulating his behavior.

Good leaders are also good teachers—perhaps not famous, but good. They are leaders who are sound in principle, persistent in purpose, and devoted to building teams. As role models, they teach with their actions and examples, always striving to impart new knowledge and improved skills to their team members. They are looked upon as masters of their disciplines, respected to advise, coach, and tutor. They are viewed as sages, wise and trusted counselors who are sought for advice and growth.

Don't be shy. Look for good mentors. That's really how we learn to lead, by watching good leaders lead (and by seeing bad leaders mess it up, probably at our expense)! In fact, leadership is *caught* more than *taught*. So seek those mentors and ask for their advice.

Spotting good mentors is easy. They usually have other junior leaders under their tutelage, preparing them to occupy positions of leadership. As do all good mentors, they pass on the lessons of their own leadership experiences in the hope that their charges won't have to experience all of the same mistakes of leading that they have encountered.

ORGANIZER

As stated earlier, good leaders are team-forgers. They realize the most valuable accomplishments are achieved by groups of well-trained people engaged in clearly defined work in which the efforts of individuals are integrated to accomplish what the individuals alone could not achieve.

Teamwork, the synergy of human organization, is largely the result of structure, coordination, and harmony. It is the leader who arranges the organizational structure, defines the lines of authority, and establishes avenues of communication that delineate the boundaries within which the team will operate. It is the leader who creates accord within the team so that team members pull together in the same direction, at the same time. It is the leader who weaves the threads of varying talents together into whole cloth which is much stronger and more useful than any of the threads alone.

It follows that good leaders must be adept at organizing and developing teams. One of the most amazing business teams ever created was Lockheed's remarkable *Skunk Works*, renowned for developing special purpose aircraft in short periods of time. Ben Rich wrote of this pioneering organization in **Skunk Works**, the story of its founder, Kelly Johnson, and his famous Lockheed team:

> *We became the most successful advanced projects company in the world by hiring talented people, paying them top dollar, and motivating them into believing that they could produce a Mach 3 airplane like the Blackbird a generation or two ahead of anybody else. Our design engineers had the keen experience to conceive the whole airplane in their mind's-eye, doing the trade-offs in their heads between aerodynamic needs and weapons requirements. We created a practical and open work environment for engineers and shop workers, forcing the guys behind the drawing boards onto the shop floor to see how their ideas were being translated into actual parts and to make any necessary changes on the spot. We made every shop worker who designed or handled a part responsible for quality control. Any worker—not just a supervisor—could send back a part that didn't meet his or her standards. That way we reduced rework and scrap waste...We encouraged*

> *our people to work imaginatively, to improvise and try unconventional approaches to problem solving, and then got out of their way. By applying the most common-sense methods to develop new technologies, we saved tremendous amounts of time and money, while operating in an atmosphere of trust and cooperation both with our government customers and between our white-collar and blue-collar employees. In the end, Lockheed's Skunk Works demonstrated the awesome capabilities of American inventiveness when free to operate under near ideal working conditions. That may be our most enduring legacy as well as our source of lasting pride.*[4]

What an extraordinary description of what leaders are supposed to do!

- Hire talented people.
- Pay them well.
- Get them to believe that they can accomplish great things.
- Establish an organizational structure in which team members are capable of (and feel responsible for) working together as a body rather than as individuals.
- Require accountability and give authority to support it.
- Encourage people to think creatively.
- Let them work.

The process is universal. The same prescription applies for leading in business, sports, or military operations.

FACILITATOR

To *facilitate* means to make something easier to perform or achieve. Kelly Johnson was a facilitator. He made his team members' jobs easier by clearing away obstacles that would otherwise impede creativity, initiative, and production. He also forced his team members to tear down the barriers between disciplines. Engineers were expected to frequent the shops and interact with the technicians who were building the parts. In so doing, they became acquainted with the production difficulties experienced by the fabricators and, coincidentally, with the fabricators' ideas for design improvement.

Removing obstacles so that team members can perform sometimes is a difficult skill for new leaders to learn. It's one of those areas in which coaching differs significantly from playing. One of the hardest transitions to make from team member to leader is to recognize that your job is now different. When you become a coach, you are no longer a player. You don't get to go out on the field and kick the ball anymore (except when demonstrating skills and techniques). Your job is to facilitate, to make things easier for the team. That doesn't mean that their work is easy. It's not; but it shouldn't be harder than necessary.

INNOVATOR

By clearing roadblocks and encouraging creativity, Kelly Johnson achieved a climate of innovation within Lockheed's *Skunk Works*. To *innovate* means to *make new*. Johnson's engineers and technicians pressed beyond the current state of aerodynamic engineering, creating new airframes, new engines, new shapes, and new skins to meet in unbelievably short time spans the needs of Lockheed's military and intelligence clients.

Ideas for improvement, however, didn't all come from group leaders. Johnson knew, that talented as they might be, his leaders would not always have the best plans. He understood that the most effective solutions often originate with team members since they are the ones most closely associated with the problems. So, he created a "practical and open work environment" in which the exchange of ideas could thrive.

PILOT

To delegate successfully, a leader must thoroughly understand the nature of power. In a team, the source of power is vested in the team members themselves. They are the strong, raw, and uncoordinated muscle of the team. Wise leaders harness and multiply team muscle through structure and orchestration,

unleashing it at critical times in proper directions for useful purposes.
In that sense, leaders are the pilots of their teams, airborne in a symbiotic relationship in which aviator and ship are mutually reliant. Pilots provide directional control to their craft, manage fuel expenditure and power settings, trim the craft for most efficient performance, and reconfigure the craft for special situations. They are vital to flight, yet no matter how skilled, pilots can't fly without their ships.

Similarly, leaders and teams are mutually reliant. Though leaders are at the helm, they need sleek, responsive teams capable of takeoff, climb, cruise, descent, and landing.

NAVIGATOR

Whether airborne or seaborne, navigators find and communicate destination and direction. They are pathfinders, knowledgeable of the objective, capable of plotting and navigating a route to the goal, aware of obstacles along the route, and sensitive to the endurance of their craft.

Leaders of teams have the same responsibilities. They must have a clear picture of where they want the team to go, a workable plan for how to get there, the ability to guide the team around inevitable obstacles, and an understanding of the team's capabilities.

DELEGATOR

Johnson and his colleagues also understood that *power* and *control* are not the same. Sometimes, leaders believe that power is acquired by being in a position to control every action of each team member. In reality, those leaders are actually made weak since they can only control the actions of the team member under scrutiny.

The most powerful leaders are those who train their team members well and then empower them to perform, a function called *delegation*. In an empowered team, team members become extensions of the leader, serving as eyes and arms and legs. The body does the bidding of the brain, but instead of every muscle move requiring a conscious impulse, the brain and nervous system act autonomically to accomplish the brain's desires.

In an empowered team, however, the team members are not blindly complying with the leader's wishes. Each team member is linked to the leader as a delegate, one who is acting on the leader's behalf. With thinking team members, the leader still serves as coach, providing guidance, instruction, and correction, but the leader is able to invest time in the facilitator function, clearing the roadway ahead to facilitate the team's progress.

LEGISLATOR

One of the difficult functions of leading is the role of legislator. In addition to setting performance standards and developing lines of communication and authority, leaders have to identify and establish boundaries and rules of play. Boundaries define the field of play and the behaviors that are acceptable during the game.

Nobody likes boundaries. They restrict action. Yet, most boundaries are established to prevent the occurrence of unfavorable events or circumstances. Coach Landry (**Landry: An Autobiography**) wrote:

> *You can't enjoy true freedom without limits. We often resent rules because they limit what we can do. Yet without rules that define a football game, you can't play the game, let alone enjoy it. The same thing is true in life.*[5]

When properly utilized, boundaries aid safe and efficient operation. For example, OSHA law regarding isolation of hazardous energy sources establishes the rules for dealing with harmful forms of energy. Past experiences in industrial operation dictated that rules be developed and codified.

The types of barriers that Kelly Johnson and his *Skunk Works* team tore down were not safety boundaries. Instead, they were unnecessary bureaucratic roadblocks that added no value to the organization and its functions. As a part of the facilitator function, leaders must always be on the lookout for rules and boundaries that unnecessarily restrict action without adding value. The boundaries must be based on reason rather than arbitrary whim. If improperly established or poorly communicated, they often become an impediment rather than an aid.

For effectiveness, boundaries should be communicated not only from the standpoint of their letter but also from the perspective of their spirit. Failure to teach the spirit or the underlying reasons for the boundaries eventually results in ignorant or malicious "compliance" with the text of the rules.

JUDGE

No team ever excels without the constant evaluation of testing, coaching, and self-analysis. Consequently, one of the most important functions of the leader is team and player evaluation.

Evaluation provides the basis for improvement. Great team performances are seldom the result of good luck; rather, they are the culmination of hard work on the practice field under the tutelage of skillful coaches who make judgments about individual and team performances and who then provide the training, teaching, and testing necessary for progress.

It seems elementary that evaluation is one of the underlying factors for improvement, yet most business organizations neither teach nor practice critical self-analysis. So, why should you? The ultimate purpose of observation and evaluation is improved performance directed at mission accomplishment. Dr. W. Edwards Deming, the father of total quality management, encouraged leaders to:

Improve constantly and forever the system of production and service. Improvement is not a one-time effort. Management is obligated to continually look for ways to reduce waste and improve quality[6]

Also, by looking, you create motivation for change, improved communication, an opportunity to correct or reinforce behaviors, and a chance to mentor.

In the role of judge, leaders sometimes have both the pleasure of praising and rewarding excellent performances and the pain of administering sanctions for undesirable behavior or poor performance. In Chapter 24 ("Disciplining the Team"), you'll find more on the discipline cycle. The negative side of the discipline cycle is, for most leaders, the hardest part of fulfilling the role of judge, but rules and boundaries that are not enforced are worse than no boundaries at all. Failure to enforce the rules dilutes all rules and disintegrates the team.

THE BOTTOM LINE

So, what's the bottom line? As a leader, you must be multi-talented since you fulfill many roles. Ultimately your job is to forge teams from the diverse talents and viewpoints of your team members. Their combined and orchestrated efforts result in great accomplishments.

LEADING PRINCIPLE

Leaders are the structural center of a team, the hub around which the organizational wheel is built. Leaders forge motivated team members into a synergistic being that is stronger by far than all of the members separately. Leaders demonstrate the behaviors and attitudes that they expect of each team member. Leaders release the energy of their teams at the right time and for the right purposes.

"Where there is no vision, the people are unrestrained ..."

(Proverbs 29:18)

Chapter 18

KNOWING YOURSELF

"We don't willingly follow leaders who don't know themselves!"

per•son•al•ity (pûr'sə-năl'ĭ-tē) *n.* **1**. The quality or fact of being a person. **2**. The totality of qualities and traits, as of character or behavior, peculiar to a specific person. **3.** The pattern of collective character, behavioral, temperamental, emotional, and mental traits of a person. **4.** Distinctive qualities of a person…

BECAUSE the effectiveness of a leader depends upon the ability to gather supporters to a cause, the personality of the leader is a key ingredient in determining how much influence that leader wields. That's why Napoleon said:

> *The personality of the general is indispensable; he is the head, he is the all of an army. The Gauls were not conquered by the Roman legion, but by Caesar. It was not before the Carthagenian soldiers that Rome was made to tremble, but before Hannibal. It was not the Macedonian phalanx which penetrated into India, but Alexander.*

Napoleon's observation about the general being "the head" and "the all" of an army may seem arrogant, appearing inappreciative of the role played by his combat soldiers, but Napoleon's experiences had taught him that, alone, highly skilled team members do not consistently conquer. Instead, team effectiveness ultimately lies in the ability of a team leader to coalesce the skills of team members into a coordinated effort yielding a synergistic result.

As we have already discovered, much of a leader's influence depends upon technical competence, a trust extended by team members to a leader because of demonstrated knowledge and skill (a form of power which we shall soon define as *expertise power*). Another portion of influence derives from the leader's character qualities of attitude and behavior, founded upon honesty and integrity, which warrant the confidence of the team (a form of power which is often accorded the title *personal power*). The personality of the leader, the nature of the person filling the leadership role, is an intangible asset which, when understood and effectively employed, has the potential for dramatically enhancing the leader's influence. Personality is the very image of a leader, a picture of human qualities etched into the minds of team members. If the image is genuine, and not feigned or contrived, the words and actions of the leader are far more believable.

BE YOURSELF!

One message, then, is clear: *Be yourself!* Don't try to be someone you are not. If you are quiet by nature, a George Patton, Jr., image isn't going to fit. Everyone will immediately know that you are acting. If you feel it necessary to fool your team members in this fashion, what else will you make up?

Herb Kelleher, the enthusiastic founder of Southwest Airlines, quipped:

> *...[A] lot of people have asked me about my leadership style—quote, unquote—and I have often said that most people who are stylish would probably not refer to it as a style, because I really don't have a leadership style except being myself.* [1]

That's precisely the point. Your leadership style is based upon your personality. If you are a quiet person, be a good, quiet leader. If you are an outgoing person, be a good, outgoing leader.

HARDWARE AND SOFTWARE

Fortunately, we are not all the same. Personalities are as different as fingerprints, and, since leadership style is based upon personality, no two leaders are exactly alike.

So, who am I? Figuring out who we are seems to take a lifetime, perhaps because we are constantly changing as we learn about ourselves. Hopefully, we grow wiser with age and experience, shedding habits which are not helpful while enhancing those that make us better citizens and humans, a process commonly called *socialization*. Socialization is the "nurture" part of "nature and nurture."

Yet no matter how hard we try, we tend to be unable to change our basic building blocks. If you are a reserved person by nature, you are unlikely to become (at least permanently) an outgoing person. We are individually hard-wired, having fundamental inclinations.

The relationship between nature and nurture is similar to the relationship between hardware and software in a computer. Computer hardware is fixed by design and construction, forming a platform for operations. Through programming and software application, the computer platform can be configured to accomplish desired tasks. Even when the hardware is lacking, enhanced software can allow the platform to perform acceptably.

Some platforms, however, no matter how good the software, are not built for certain tasks. Similarly, no one personality can optimally accomplish all leadership chores. There *are* situations for which a George Patton, Jr., is the best leadership personality.

BORN OR MADE?

The hardware-software analogy sheds light on the question of whether great leaders are born or made. The answer, of course, is that great leaders are both born *and* made. Michael Jordan would neither have become the basketball sensation he was without much God-given talent, nor excelled without superb coaching from mentors like Dean Smith, revered University of North Carolina basketball mentor.

Not everyone can be a great basketball player because not everyone has exceptional athletic talent, nor can every person be a great leader since exceptional talent is necessary in that endeavor as well. Yet most people can be taught the rudiments of basketball and can perform at a useful level. Similarly, most people can learn leadership fundamentals, applying them in a workman-like fashion. (In fact, most people *must* perform as leaders! What greater leadership task is there than raising children?)

Furthermore, one doesn't need to be the best player in order to be the best coach. Great personal talent may, in some cases, be a disadvantage to a leader. In **Paterno By the Book**, Coach Joe Paterno wrote:

> *Sometimes a terrific player who becomes a coach doesn't get it straight that he's there not because he knows how to do it, but because he's supposed to teach it. I once had a guy on the staff who had just finished a career as a great kicker and punter. Everybody said, What a great punting coach he's going to be. This kicker was the lousiest punting coach I ever saw. Why? He kept punting and thought it was teaching. He should have kicked once, and let the kid do it ten times. Maybe the rule is that a coach shouldn't enjoy playing as much as he enjoys teaching.*[2]

So, the best leaders are often great teachers who recognize their limitations, surround themselves with talented people, train them to function well in their roles as team members, and then let them play.

DIVIDING THE PERSONALITY

Personality typing is not new. Socrates, Plato, and Aristotle all found value in categorizing and reading the personalities of people. Over two millennia ago, Hippocrates, the father of modern medicine, divided the personalities of people into four types: *choleric*—the goal oriented, outgoing, driving personality; *sanguine*—the passionate, fun-loving, affectionate personality; *phlegmatic*—the peaceful, patient, people-oriented personality; and *melancholic*—the critical, brooding, exacting introvert. Many of today's personality typing tools are enhanced variations of Hippocrates' model.

Isabel Myers and Kathryn Briggs extended the work of Dr. Carl Jung, dividing the personality into spectrums of *Introvert vs. Extrovert, Sensing vs. Intuitive, Thinking vs. Feeling,* and *Judging vs. Perceiving*. Through the work of David Keirsey (**Please Understand Me II**), modern meaning has been added to the Myers-Briggs Type Indicator, still an excellent tool for personality analysis.

The facets of personality seem almost limitless. The Minnesota Multiphasic Personality Inventory (MMPI) samples many elements of personality and is widely used in industry, especially for determining the suitability of job applicants as security risks.

TASK VS. PEOPLE

One obvious way of dividing the personality is to distinguish between those for whom goals are most important versus those for whom people are most important. In Chapter 20 (Balancing People and Production), we will briefly review the work of Drs. Robert R. Blake and Jane S. Mouton. In their Managerial Grid® (See Figure 20-2), leadership styles are identified by attitudes and behaviors that illustrate a *concern for production* over a *concern for people* or vice versa. For Blake and Mouton, the balance between those two factors is the most rudimentary divide of personality.

So, how do personalities of those two inclinations differ? In our leadership courses, we often ask class members to identify typical characteristics of those who are task-oriented versus people-oriented. The lists include descriptive terms like the ones illustrated in Figure 18-1 (Task vs. People). Basic differences are, unsurprisingly, that task-oriented people focus first on objectives and then on people, whereas human concerns are of greatest import to the people-oriented and goal accomplishment is seen as an outgrowth of properly training and caring for team members.

Figure 18-1 Task vs. People

RATIONAL VS. EMOTIONAL

Another common personality divide separates the rational personality from the emotional personality. The rational ("left-brained") person seems to view the world with greater emphasis upon facts, data, and objectivity. The emotional ("right-brained") person, however, relies more heavily upon intuition, feeling, and subjectivity. We should be careful here to avoid giving the impression that rational thinkers are devoid of emotion. As David Keirsey makes clear in **Please Understand Me II**, rationals are not without emotion; rather, they are more reserved in demonstrating emotion than their right-brained, intuitive counterparts.[3] We all seem to be emotional creatures at the core.

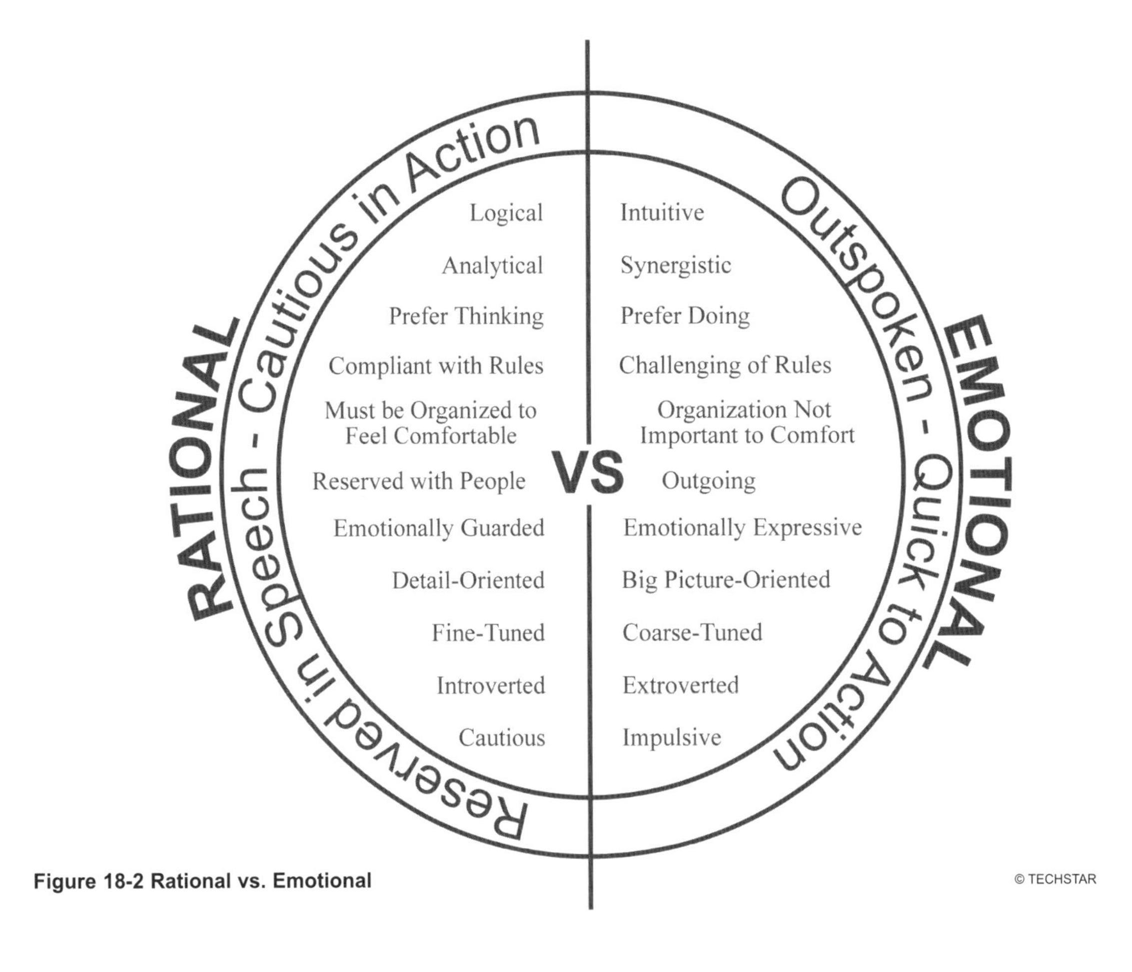

Figure 18-2 Rational vs. Emotional

When asked to describe the characteristics of rationals versus emotionals, our class members typically differentiate the two with terms similar to those illustrated in Figure 18-2 (Rational vs. Emotional). Emotional personalities are inclined to be outspoken and quick to action, whereas rational personalities are more cautious and thoughtful before acting and reserved in speech.

FOUR BASIC QUADRANTS

By integrating these two basic personality divides (See Figure 18-3, Four Basic Quadrants), we can identify, at least in general terms, a person who is emotionally expressive and goal-oriented (Quadrant 1), another inclined to be emotionally expressive and people-oriented (Quadrant 2), a third who tends to be emotionally reserved and people-oriented (Quadrant 3), and a fourth who is emotionally reserved and goal-oriented (Quadrant 4).

For Hippocrates, Quadrant 1 would correspond to the *Choleric*, Quadrant 2 to the *Sanguine*, Quadrant 3 to the *Phlegmatic*, and Quadrant 4 to the *Melancholic*. In the DiSC® Classic Personal Profile System, Quadrant 1 inclines toward *Dominance* (D), Quadrant 2 toward *Influence* (I), Quadrant 3 toward *Steadiness* (S), and Quadrant 4 toward *Conscientiousness* (C).[4] Similar comparisons can be drawn

Figure 18-3 Four Basic Quadrants

regarding combinations of the personality spectrums of the Myers-Briggs Type Indicator and other typing tools.

A caution is in order at this point. Personalities are usually far more complex than can be expressed by a system of categories. Our experience with typing personalities indicates that few people fall into a single quadrant. Instead, personalities are more like cake recipes containing a bit of this and a bit of that. Some cakes have more flour, others more sugar, and yet others more eggs. Personality typing tools simply help us to understand our ingredients and complexity a little better.

PERSONALITY TYPES

In Figure 18-4, Quadrant Characteristics, we have recorded personality traits which we have found to be representative of the respective quadrants. For example,

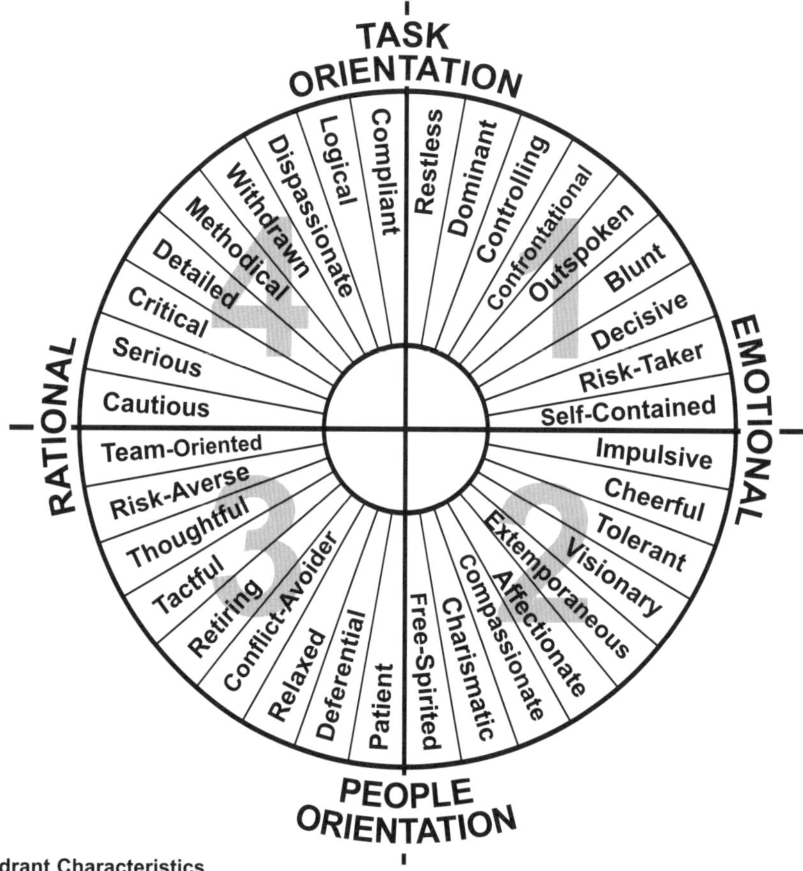

Figure 18-4 Quadrant Characteristics

Quadrant 1 personalities are emotionally expressive, task-oriented people. Hippocrates' *Cholerics*, they are frequently restless and impatient, especially with people. They tend to be dominant and controlling (like an alpha male or female), taking charge of problems and other team members. They are usually unafraid of confrontation and are outspoken and blunt in speech. Typically, they are very decisive, taking less time than other personalities to evaluate problems and decide on solutions. They are less afraid of risk and wish to go straight to the implementation stage of problem-solving. They also seem to be less needy of others, being self-contained and well-equipped to operate on their own. They are ruled by a desire for *dominance* and *control*. They are WARRIORS. (See Figure 18-5, *TECHSTAR* Personality Types.)

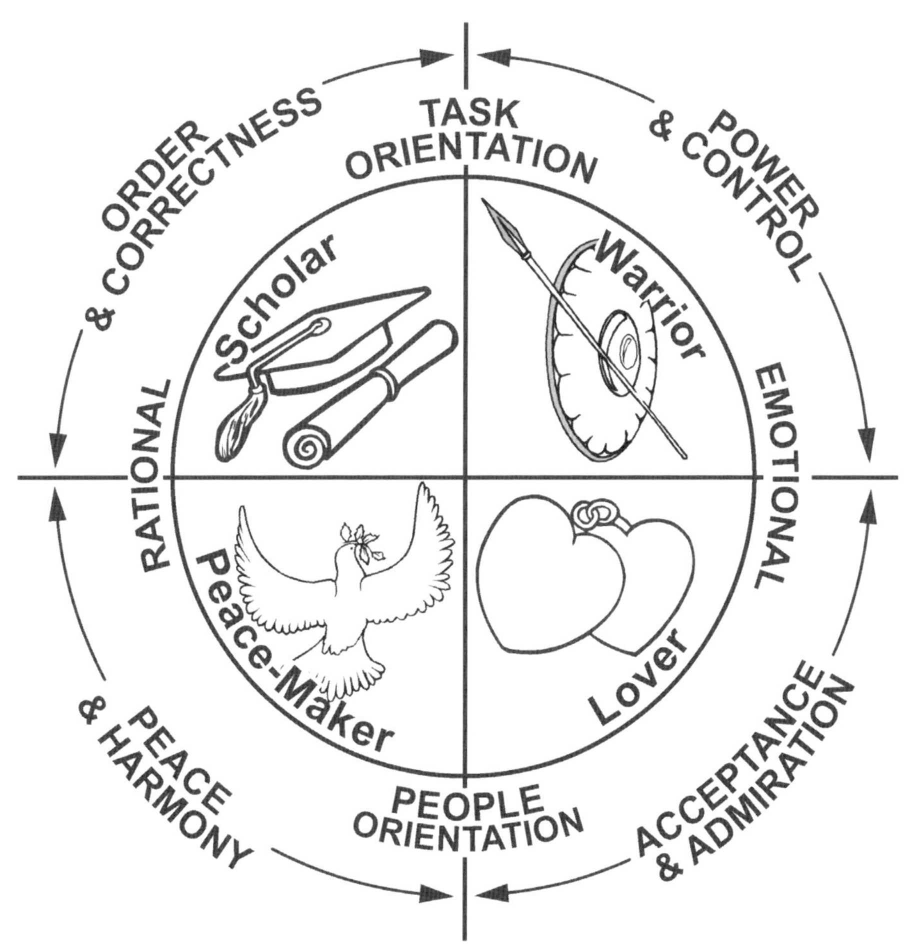

Figure 18-5 *TECHSTAR* Personality Types

Quadrant 2 personalities are emotionally expressive, people-oriented souls. Hippocrates' *Sanguines*, they are inclined to be free-spirited and impulsive, often unconstrained by organizational or societal rules. Yet they tend to be forgiven for skirting the boundaries since they are so friendly, cheerful, and attractive—charismatics who rely upon their "shiny" personalities to make relational inroads and influence others. Quadrant 2 personalities are usually affectionate, having in return a high need for affection. They are spontaneous in action, compassionate in nature, and tolerant of others. They are ruled by a desire for *acceptance* and *admiration*. They are LOVERS.

Quadrant 3 personalities are rational, emotionally restrained, people-oriented individuals. Hippocrates' *Phlegmatics*, they possess the counseling characteristics. They are tactful, patient, deferential, and objective, especially when dealing with others. Their personalities are relaxed, peace-loving, and conflict-averse, given to solving problems through dialogue and compromise in a quiet, unemotional manner. They are ruled by a desire for *peace* and *harmony*. They are PEACE-MAKERS.

Quadrant 4 personalities are rational, emotionally restrained, task-oriented people. Akin to Hippocrates' *Melancholics*, they are detailed, methodical, and dispassionate, possessing an extreme sense of justice and fairness. Serious and cautious by nature, they are unusually well-equipped to critically evaluate and assess problems in a logical way, sometimes seeming almost detached or withdrawn from the people-side of problems. Opposite from their sanguine counterparts, well-defined boundaries and rule compliant behavior are important to Quadrant 4 personalities. Though rational in their approach to problem-solving, they are certainly not devoid of emotion. Their heightened sense of justice and fairness is easily offended, leading to bouts of brooding. Since they are ruled by a desire for *order* and *correctness*, they critically observe and assess the tiniest imperfections, both in their environment and in others, sometimes a very annoying trait! They are SCHOLARS.

PERSONALITY MAPPING

By combining the personality divides of "Task vs. People" and "Rational vs. Emotional," we have a simple tool for categorizing the personalities of the people with whom we interact (and also of ourselves). The resulting *TECHSTAR* Personality Map is illustrated in Figure 18-6. It incorporates quadrant characteristics to help determine how much of your personality is WARRIOR, LOVER, PEACE-MAKER, and SCHOLAR. Appendix A (Personality

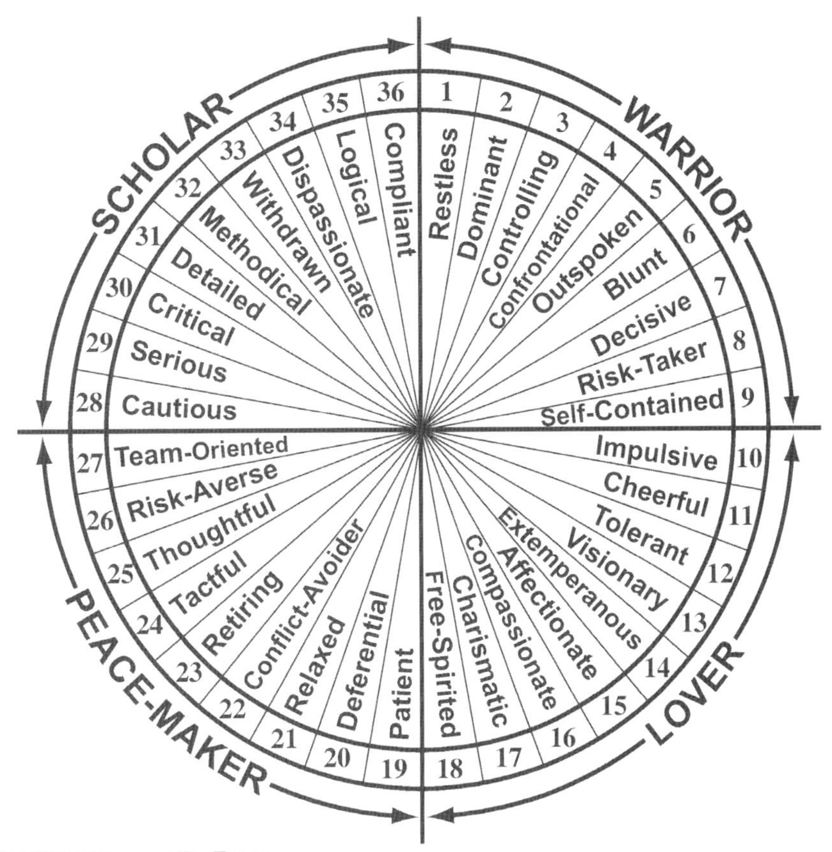

Figure 18-6 ***TECHSTAR*** **Personality Types**

© TECHSTAR

Questionnaire) contains an uncomplicated questionnaire that will help you complete the *TECHSTAR* Personality Scorecard (See Figure 18-7). By mapping yourself and then having others map you as they see you, you can acquire a more objective picture of your own personality traits.

READING PERSONALITIES

So what is the value in reading and typing personalities? Sun Tzu said, "Know the enemy and know yourself; in a hundred battles you will never be in peril."[5] First, as Sun Tzu admonished, we become far better acquainted with our own tendencies, strengths, and weaknesses. We learn who we are, how we are apt to act and speak under certain conditions, and where we are susceptible to failure. Second, we are far less surprised by the actions and words of others. In dealing with a WARRIOR, we neither will be taken aback when that person doesn't interact in a tactful manner, nor will we be startled by the critical spirit of the SCHOLAR. Best of all, we will be better equipped to forecast roles in which our team members are likely to best perform.

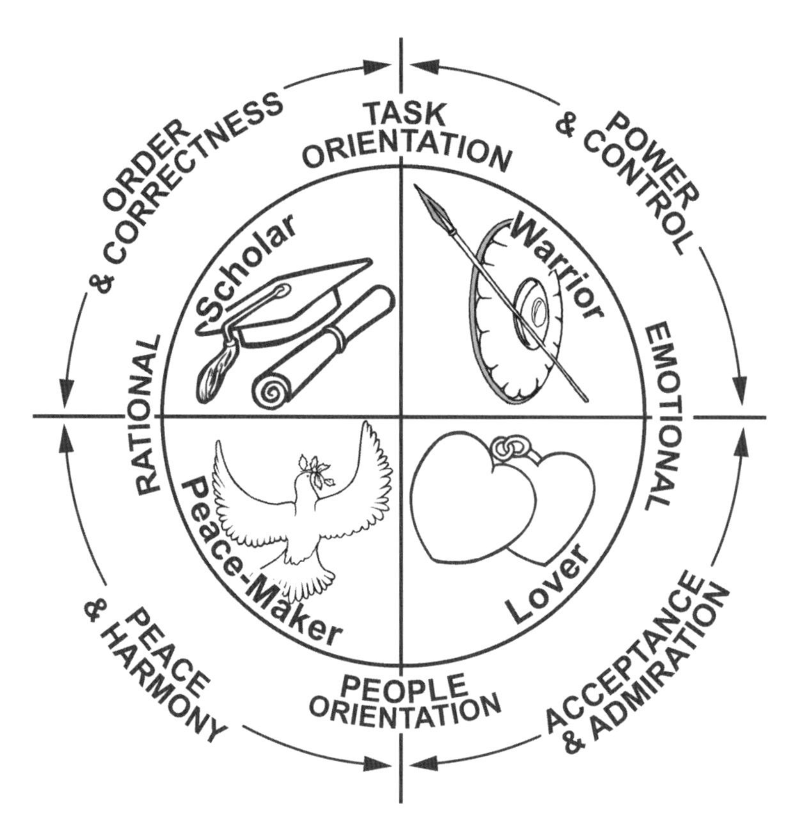

Figure 18-7 ***TECHSTAR*** **Personality Scorecard** © TECHSTAR

THE BOTTOM LINE

So, what's the bottom line? You're not going to change the "hardware" portion of the personalities of your people; but by knowing them better, you can tune their "software" to support the team. Further, by knowing yourself, you'll know what areas of your life need work.

> **LEADING PRINCIPLE** Personality is the image of a leader, a picture of human qualities etched into the minds of team members. If the image is genuine, not feigned or contrived, the words and actions of the leader are far more believable. So, be yourself! If God made you an outgoing person, be a good outgoing leader. If He crafted you as a quiet person, then be a good quiet leader.

"Know the enemy and know yourself;
in a hundred battles you will never be in peril."

(Sun Tzu, 500 B.C.)

Chapter 19

Motivating The Team

"We don't willingly follow leaders who don't understand us!"

mo•tive (mō'tĭv) *n.* **1.** An emotion, desire, physiological need, or similar impulse that acts as an incitement to action.

mo•ti•vate.(mō'tə-vāt') *tr.v.* **1.** To provide with an incentive; move to action; impel.

HUMANS seemed predisposed to avoid change. We love security, habits, and unrocked boats. Yet accomplishment (whether individual or organizational) always demands change. Consequently, the conspicuous problem of leaders—in fact, the very essence of leadership—is to impel people toward new thoughts and behaviors, while reinforcing the habits and actions that have proven indispensable to mission accomplishment.

This force for constant renewal, a process as important to organizations as cell renewal is to the body, seldom occurs without visionary leaders who recognize the necessity for change. Great leaders, then, are invariably distinguished by an uncanny ability to motivate people. Vince Lombardi, legendary head coach of the Green Bay Packers, cautioned:

> *Coaches who can outline plays on a blackboard are a dime a dozen. The ones who win get inside their players and motivate them.*

Lombardi makes it clear that it's not enough to know the plays. You must instill a desire to perform in your team members.

The desire to perform can be driven by either of two opposing forces. Napoleon Bonaparte, one of history's renowned motivators, summarized these two forces succinctly: "There are two levers for moving men—interest and fear."

Interest is *want-to* motivation; fear is *have-to* motivation. As we learned in the first chapter, they are often identified as *intrinsic* and *extrinsic* motivators—from within and from without.

HAVE-TO MOTIVATION

The forces of fear and interest are both legitimate and useful tools. Yet, as with all tools, there is a right way and a wrong way to use them. If improperly employed, either can cut in the wrong direction. Wise leaders know when, and in what proportion, to use each.

Lombardi, renowned head coach of Green Bay during their years of domination, used a heavy dose of fear motivation. Tom Landry observed Lombardi's methods firsthand:

> *One way to motivate people is by using emotion. Vince Lombardi was a master of fear motivation. His players knew if they didn't perform they would pay the price of a tongue-lashing, extra work, or some other punitive indication of Vince's disfavor.*[1]

But Landry also saw the tightrope Lombardi walked in employing fear motivation:

> *I believe fear motivation is always risky. It worked for Vince in Green Bay during the sixties because he had the talent to win. The negative sense of suffering Vince put the Packers through forced them to bond together as a group; when they won, the players forged a powerful sense of attachment to their teammates. What could easily have turned to hatred for Lombardi turned to love in the wake of victory—winning made it all worth it. But if you don't win, fear motivation quickly backfires. There's no payoff to make players feel it's "worth it."* [2]

"Stonewall" Jackson (Robert E. Lee's brilliant Second Corps Commander in the Army of Northern Virginia) got by with it; George S. Patton, Jr. (Commander of the unexcelled Third Army), got by with it; Hyman Rickover (father of the U.S. Naval Nuclear Propulsion Program) got by with it; and Bobby Knight (Coach of the famed Indiana Hoosiers and now with Texas Tech) gets by with it. Why? Because all their teams were (are) winners. Their eccentricities are forgiven in the wake of their successes, but their people tend to polarize into two camps: they either love their leaders or hate them depending, for the most part, upon how they have personally been treated by the leader.

The lesson is that if you intend to use fear motivation as a steady diet, you'd better be a strategic and tactical genius. Most of us don't measure up. We need to balance *have-to* and *want-to*. In fairness, historical readings of most of the leaders just mentioned show that they also balanced the two forces. It's just that their medicine, especially in the formative stages of their organizations, was so strong that the lasting stories surrounding their reputations inevitably focus on their toughness. Beneath their gruff exteriors beat softer hearts for which other less known stories abound.

Anyone who has been on the receiving end of fear motivation knows the anxiety it causes. It's not a pleasant feeling, and the distaste for that feeling may lead to the unwarranted conclusion that fear motivation should never be used. On the contrary, for some circumstances, fear is exactly the right medicine.

When Patton took over Second Corps in Tunisia (March, 1943), he relieved a commander, Lloyd Fredendall, who had served the unit poorly. Just a few weeks earlier, in their first major engagement, Second Corps had been defeated at the hands of Erwin Rommel at Kasserine Pass, suffering extensive casualties and equipment losses. The unit was demoralized and ill-prepared to continue. Yet, they had to continue. Patton had less than two weeks to prepare them for combat. As a unit, they were not ready for a dose of purely want-to motivation. So Patton mixed his rousing unit talks and visits with a healthy measure of fear. Carlo D'Este, author of the Patton biography **Patton: A Genius for War**, described the medicine and its effect:

> *Patton had only ten days to make his presence felt before the corps was to open a diversionary offensive...to threaten Rommel's flank... Discipline in II Corps was nonexistent... [Patton] ruthlessly used shock tactics to cajole, bully, encourage, and excite his men into believing that they were capable of defeating their enemy. Patton seemed to be everywhere at once, using every leadership stratagem learned during his thirty-four-year military career. Uniform regulations were strictly enforced, and offenders punished with fines, many nabbed personally by Patton. Though seemingly trivial, even nonessential, what Bradley called Patton's "spit and polish" reign had a badly needed positive effect.*[3]

So, when *should* fear be used as a motivator? When time is short, when team members are lethargic, when the consequences of failure are high, when performance is significantly below standard: these are conditions which may dictate the use of fear motivation. Always remember, the purpose in using fear to motivate must ultimately be to serve the team to make it a better unit, not as a means to self-aggrandize. Even Patton mixed it with encouragement, challenge, and praise of individual team members who were performing in exemplary fashion.

WANT-TO MOTIVATION

Fear motivation is useful for turning individuals and organizations from poor habits and old, destructive ways, but it is, at best, a short-term tool. Further, it requires that a strong coercive power base be available. Otherwise, the tactic is little more than an idle threat.

Ultimately, *want-to* motivation is the only method for achieving Olympic-level performance. Consider Olympic gymnast Shannon Miller, a top athlete who accumulated more Olympic gymnastic medals than any other American female competitor. Could she have been coerced into such high-level achievements? Our own experiences convince us of the foolishness of such a proposition. Superior performance comes from an internal desire, not an external force. *Have-to* motivation may be useful to get us started, but it can't sustain performance.

So, where does *want-to* motivation come from? Predominantly, it comes from pride in personal and team performance, the legitimacy of individual and team goals (from which such pride ensues when goals are accomplished), and a belief in the ability of the team's leader to orchestrate the individual efforts to accomplish team goals.

There is perhaps no better example of a *want-to* motivator than Robert E. Lee, Commander of the Army of Northern Virginia. Lee biographer, Douglas Southall Freeman, recorded the effect of Lee on his army:

> *All that can be said of Lee's dealings with his officers can be said in even warmer tones of his relations with the men in the ranks. They were his chief pride, his first obligation. Their distress was his deepest concern, their well-being his constant aim. His manner with them was said by his lieutenants to be perfect. Never ostentatious or consciously dramatic, his bearing, his record*

> *of victories, his manifest interest in the individual, and his conversation with the humblest private he met in the road combined to create in the minds of his troops a reverence, a confidence, and an affection that built up the morale of the army. And that morale was one of the elements that contributed most to his achievements. The men came to believe that whatever he did was right—that whatever he assigned them they could accomplish. Once that belief became fixed, the Army of Northern Virginia was well-nigh invincible. There is, perhaps, no more impressive example in modern war of the power of personality in creating morale.*[4]

Lee had at his command the ability to coerce. Yet, he used it sparingly, relying instead upon the extraordinary power of his reputation, acquired through demonstrated expertise, and a remarkable ability to treat others with respect despite his high station. He knew that what he asked his soldiers to do could not be achieved simply through an order. As a consequence, the esteem in which he was regarded by generals and privates alike was reverential.

President Lincoln also knew of the power of *want-to* motivation. In 1842, he spoke to a gathering of temperance workers, admonishing them of the need for persuasion over force:

> *When the conduct of men is designed to be influenced, persuasion, kind, unassuming persuasion, should ever be adopted. It is an old and a true maxim "that a drop of honey catches more flies than a gallon of gall." So with men. If you would win a man to your cause, "first" convince him that you are his sincere friend. Therein is a drop of honey that catches his heart, which, say what he will, is the great high road to his reason, and which, once gained, you will find but little trouble in convincing his judgment of the justice of your cause, if indeed that cause really be a just one. On the contrary, assume to dictate to his judgment, or to command his action, or to mark him as one to be shunned and despised, and he will retreat within himself, close all the avenues to his head and his heart... Such is man, and so must he be understood by those who would lead him, even to his own best interest.*[5]

Some say that Mr. Lincoln was too forbearing, too soft, too patient. Yet, it was, for the most part, his decisions, in a principled struggle to restore the union, that resulted in the deaths of 620,000 Americans in the bloodiest conflict of our nation's history. He was both hard and soft. He could use force when compelled, but he preferred reason.

A REASON FOR ACTION

Reason is an appeal to the rational side. An old American saying warns that *a man convinced against his will is of the same opinion still*. Force can change a behavior temporarily, but, in the absence of force, behaviors tend to revert to previous forms. No permanent change occurs.

When leaders rely on force (*have-to* motivation) they must be able to bring that force to bear at all times. They are doomed to watch their people incessantly. Moreover, people who are motivated only by fear adopt a posture of sullen compliance, an attitude of, "I'll do exactly what you tell me to—and not a damned thing more." The result is individual survivalism, not cohesive team performance.

Instead, teams need people who are *self-motivated*, motivated from the inside, not the outside. In a *Readers Digest* article entitled "Why Russia Can't Feed Itself," October, 1989, author David Satter recounts a tale of Russian farmers plowing their fields erratically—nine inches deep at the edges in accordance with regulation, but only one or two inches deep toward the centers. The author learned that their behavior was shaped by how far into the fields the state inspectors walked. The Russian farmers had become motivated by a desire to *finish*, not *accomplish*. They were doing only enough to get by. They had no personal stake in the activity, aside from avoiding punishment.[6]

That's the result of habitual *have-to* motivation. At its worst, it is simply punishment avoidance. Its accomplishments are too often superficial and seldom lasting. Indeed, the Soviet experiment, dead in under a century, is perhaps the world's greatest monument to unremitting *have-to* motivation best summarized by the Russian workers themselves: *They pretend to pay us, and we pretend to work!*

Self-motivated performance (performance that does not require constant watching) is not possible without a belief in what you are doing. Team members need to believe in something, something that makes sense, to become self-motivated. They need a purpose for extending their best efforts, especially when personal sacrifice for the sake of a team is demanded. They are capable of bearing much for a goal in which they believe. Nietzche said, "He who has a *why* to live can bear with almost any *how*."

Accordingly, *Why?* is the fundamental building block of *want-to* motivation. The answer to *Why?* is what changes attitudes, the seeds of behaviors. Behavioral psychologists have long taught us that behaviors cannot be changed permanently without changes in the attitudes that motivate them.

It seems clear that, just to have a shot at long-term success, leaders must eventually provide satisfying answers to the unasked question, "Why should I work hard (and intelligently) for this team and its coach?" Leaders bear a heavy responsibility to ensure that team members understand the goals of the team *and the reasons for the goals*. In the absence of such an understanding, a team in its true sense probably cannot be assembled.

WINNING MOTIVATES

Nothing answers the question of *Why?* better than winning itself. Through winning, team members acquire a solid understanding of how team success nourishes the team members individually. Many of Patton's soldiers hated him, at least in the beginning (*Our blood, his guts!*); but they learned, under Patton, that they won. More casualties inflicted, fewer casualties accepted. That's why tough leaders like "Stonewall" Jackson, Patton, Rickover, and Bobby Knight are forgiven for their rough edges. Though their team members don't like their methods, their teams win, and through winning, team members discover *want-to* motivation. It matters less how it is learned than that it is learned! That's one of the reasons that leadership style is subordinate to leadership principles.

SOMETIMES I NEED A PUSH

Winning—that best of motivators—doesn't just happen. It's usually the result of immense effort, accompanied by discomfort and change, conditions which most of us avoid when possible. (Have you ever met a person who, *without prior training*, was able to chart a course through acute adversity in pursuit of a goal? That ability seems absent in the natural man. It is taught. How many people do you know who could put themselves through a Marine boot camp?)

So, given the human tendency to validate Isaac Newton's First Law of Motion (a body at rest tends to stay at rest), how do you teach the taste of winning? The answer is found in the adage: *Action precedes motivation*.

Sometimes we need a push to get going. Just as eagles teach their young to fly by shoving them out of the nest, so must leaders sometimes thrust their "young" into flying situations. The push may be intimidating. It may cause fear. We may not like it at the time, but if it's done for the right reason in the right way, we get a taste of flying! Once we experience the pride of accomplishment, we begin to understand its value. We begin to understand why that mean old coach was pushing so hard! Benjamin Disraeli, former Prime Minister of the United Kingdom said, “Action may not always bring happiness; but there is no happiness without action.”

Again, caution is in order. Power is intoxicating. Some leaders enjoy pushing for the sake of pushing. That's the wrong motivation. Eagles don't push their young out of the nest for fun, and when they do, they fly beneath them to make sure they don't hit the ground!

THE ABILITY TO INSPIRE

Pushes are sometimes necessary, especially in the training phases of teams, but at the heart of leadership, is the ability to inspire team members. It's what Lombardi meant when he said that real leaders get inside their people and motivate them.

THE BOTTOM LINE

So, what's the bottom line? If your organization is dead, guess whose job it is to *INSPIRE* it? Motivation begins with YOU!!

LEADING PRINCIPLE

Have-to motivation and *want-to* motivation are both legitimate tools, but they have different purposes. The former is a turning tool. The latter is the only tool that can ultimately take you and your team to Olympic-level performance. Great leaders know how and when to use each tool.

Chapter 20

Balancing People And Production

"We don't willingly follow leaders who don't challenge us!"

chal•lenge (chăl'ənj) *n.* **1a.** A call to engage in a contest, fight, or competition. **b.** An act or statement of defiance; a call to confrontation. **2.** A demand for explanation or justification; a calling into question. **3.** A sentry's call… **4.** A test of one's abilities or resources.

FOR eaglets, learning to fly must be frightening, difficult, and filled with risk. Some must surely be lost in the process. Yet, if they can't fly, they can't survive.

In many ways, leaders face the same dilemma in training and leading teams. On the one hand, they must perpetually push their teams toward higher standards of performance; but, on the other, they must reassure their teams through training, coaching, and encouragement that they have a high probability of succeeding, and that the rewards are worth the risk. It's a dichotomy that is seldom easy and never devoid of risk—two forces that seem to pull in opposite directions. It is the resolution of these two forces that leads to superior performance.

A TIMELESS PRESCRIPTION

Do you remember your mathematical study of vector analysis and force resolution? We learned that when two or more forces act upon an object at the same time (but in different directions), the forces are resolved into one, and the object responds as if to a single force.

Of course, orchestrating human performance and persuading team members to act in concert to accomplish difficult tasks isn't as simple as vector resolution! Nevertheless, leaders throughout the ages have learned that these two forces—1) establishing high standards while, at the same time, 2) coaching teams how to meet those standards—is a prescription for achieving superior performance. (See Figure 20-1, Coaching for Superior Performance.)

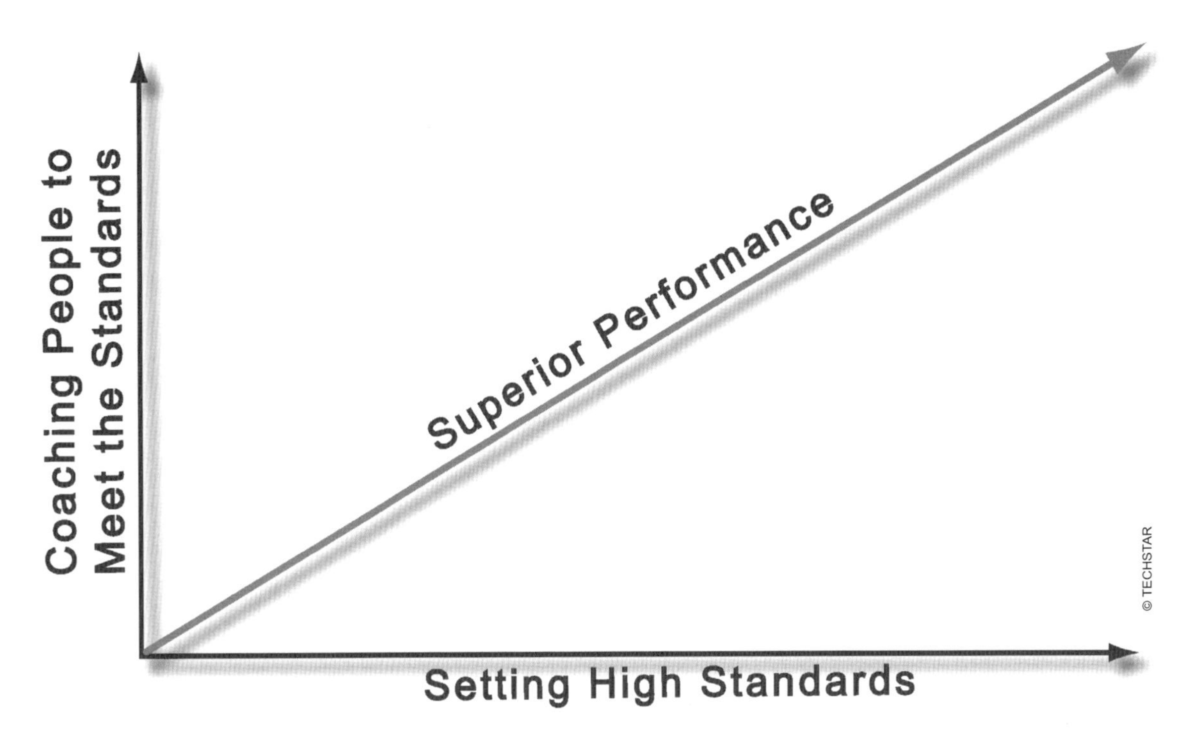

Figure 20-1 Coaching for Superior Performance

Sun Tzu (**Sun Tzu: The Art of War**) captured this essential formula in his advice to other leaders:

> *Regard your soldiers as your children, and they will follow you into the deepest valleys; look upon them as your own beloved sons, and they will stand by you even until death. If, however, you are indulgent, but unable to make authority felt; kind-hearted, but unable to enforce your commands; and incapable, moreover, of quelling disorder, then your soldiers must be likened to spoiled children. They are useless for any practical purpose.*

This great Chinese philosopher and general describes a leader who is strict and demanding, yet loving and compassionate toward his people, just as if they were his own children. It is the combination of these two qualities that inspires a team to "follow you into the deepest valleys."

We see exactly those qualities in Coach Norman Dale (Gene Hackman) as he reforms the Hickory Huskers into a championship team in the movie, **Hoosiers**. Or Joe Clark (Morgan Freeman) in his approach to revitalizing East Side High in Patterson, New Jersey, portrayed on screen in the movie, **Lean on Me**. Or Jaimé

Escalante (Edward James Olmos) in his quest to inspire the kids of Garfield High School in Los Angeles toward earning a college education in **Stand and Deliver**. Or Brigadier General Frank Savage (Gregory Peck) as he rebuilds the 918th Bomb Group in the movie, **Twelve O'Clock High**. In every case, the leaders were tough and demanding with their teams (perhaps even coercive in the beginning), yet their relationships with their teams grew to one of profound respect, appreciation, and love. Remember what Coach Dale said to his team before the state finals? "I love you guys." Only movies, you say? Three are based, in part, on true stories. All provide us with clear visual examples of the effect of great leaders on their teams, a story that is acted out on life's stage everyday throughout the world.

BLAKE/MOUTON MANAGERIAL GRID

Tough and tender. How can a leader be both? Between 1950 and 1980, Robert R. Blake and Jane S. Mouton worked extensively studying leaders, leadership styles, and the parameters that leaders value as they lead their teams. Two factors, above all others, emerged from their studies that differentiated leadership styles. One was *concern for production* and the other was *concern for people*. Blake and Mouton juxtaposed these two factors in a two-dimensional, segmented grid pattern that they called **The Managerial Grid®**.[2] (See Figure 20-2, **The Managerial Grid®**.) Do you see the similarity with the concept of force resolution that we just discussed? The *concern for production* axis correlates with setting high standards, while the *concern for people* axis corresponds to coaching teams how to meet the standards.

Blake and Mouton then developed a method to categorize the styles of leaders within the grid pattern. For example, a leader who cared nine segments for production, but only one segment for people was categorized as a (9,1) leader. The Blake/Mouton studies found that leaders with this style tend to rely upon pushing or coercion—force of will—to accomplish their objectives. As a result, the style was called an *authority-obedience* management style. It's not wrong to be (9,1), but the style has clear limits of value. In the hands of a self-serving leader, an unhealthy desire for personal power may become more important than objective accomplishment.

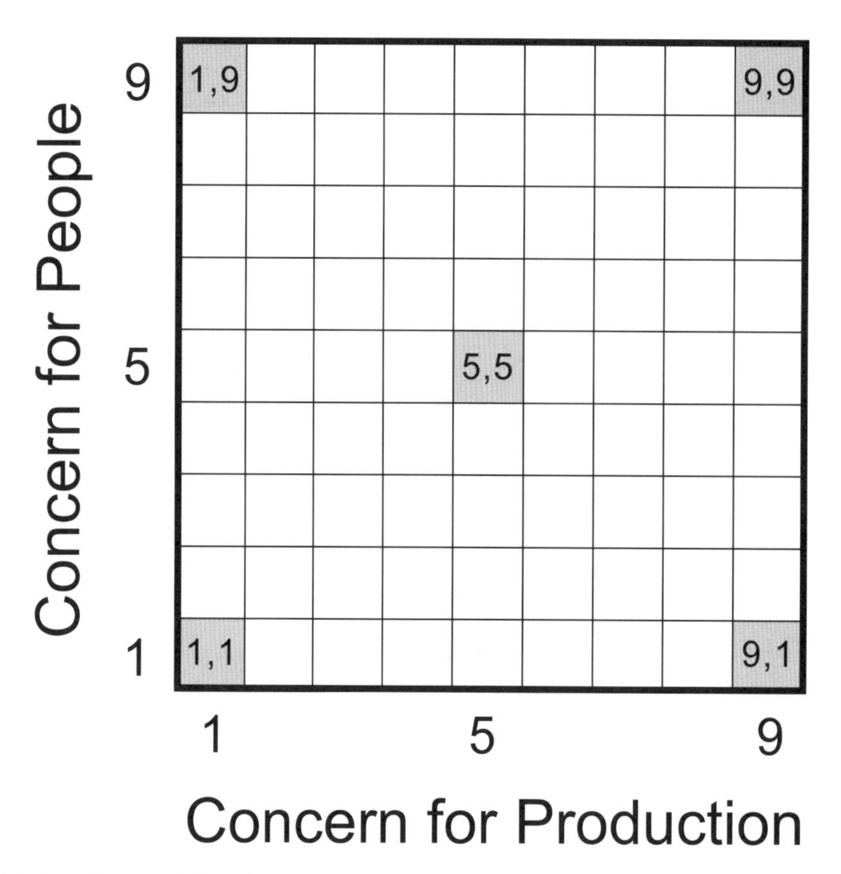

Figure 20-2 The Managerial Grid®

At the opposite corner, Blake and Mouton identified a 1,9 style in which the leader cared nine segments for people, but only one segment for production. Blake and Mouton termed this the *country club* style of management. Persuasion (pulling) is this leader's primary tool. Again, it's not a wrong style, but, alone, it seldom raises a team to high levels of performance. Further, an unhealthy tendency may develop if popularity becomes the leader's true motive. If so, it is as self-serving a motive as the *authority-obedience* leader's need for power. In fact, it is probably the same need displayed in a different form.

The central finding of the Blake/Mouton studies is that neither style in the extreme—(9,1) nor (1,9)—produced ideal long-term results. Rather, a combination of the two, a balance between concern for production and caring for people, shone as the most effective method for leading teams toward superior performance. Blake and Mouton termed this (9,9) style of leadership the *team management* style. We must both set high standards and, at the same time, care deeply about our team members in coaching them toward success if we expect them to achieve Olympic-level feats.

A caution is in order at this point. The *team management* (9,9) style is *not* appropriate for every situation. Different situations require different medicine. (This is something you know from raising your kids!) Though the (9,9) style is what Blake and Mouton advocated as a leadership lifestyle, they recognized that individual leadership situations sometimes dictate the use of other team tactics. For example, a (9,1) approach may, in perspective, be the kindest and wisest tool for a leader where rapid change is necessary to the team's survival. It may not feel good to the team members at the time, but it is ultimately in their own best interests. (Patton's takeover of Second Corps in North Africa after the Kasserine Pass debacle in 1943 is a good example.) Other situations may require a leader to use an opposite (1,9) approach, to be a nurturer to the team. Reading situations and deciphering the best medicine to apply is one of the most demanding parts of leading.

Blake's and Mouton's studies are not the only confirmation of the need to set high standards and then to coach team members toward goal accomplishment while demonstrating care. In 1939, Kurt Lewin, a prominent Austrian psychologist, led a now-famous study in leadership style. The experiment monitored the behavior of three groups of boys as they were sequentially led by three teachers, all employing different leadership styles. One acted the authoritarian (the 9,1 leader); another the *laissez faire* "hands-off" leader (1,1); and the third an involved, coaching leader (9,9). Under the authoritarian, the boys worked diligently, but only when the teacher was present. Under the *laissez faire* leader, the boys accomplished the least, produced the lowest quality of work, and demonstrated the lowest level of motivation. When the teacher was absent, they did little. Under the coaching style leader, a teacher who challenged the boys with high standards while actively teaching and encouraging them to find and implement solutions, the boys produced the best quality work with the greatest level of creativity. With the encouragement and direction of their leader, they found new ways to do things. Moreover, they continued to work while their mentor was not present.[3]

Though our business teams are not comprised of children, Lewin's experiments validate some important lessons that each of us has learned about ourselves and the organizations in which we work. We want to contribute. We want to be allowed to find intelligent, effective ways of doing things. We realize that we don't know everything about our jobs and thus need guidance. We know that, to improve, we need to be compared against legitimate—and often rising—standards. In that endeavor, we want to be led by skillful, knowledgeable mentors who will both challenge us to do better and then teach us how!

THE BOTTOM LINE

So, what's the bottom line? Superior performance is not a likely outcome for your team unless you do two things: 1) demand high standards of performance, and 2) teach the team how to achieve those standards. If you don't do both, your fledglings are not going to fly!

LEADING PRINCIPLE	Leaders must perpetually push their teams toward higher standards of performance while, at the same time, reassuring them of the probability of success through training, coaching and encouragement, forces that seem to pull in opposite directions. It is the resolution of these two forces that leads to superior performance.

Chapter 21

Caring For The Team

"We don't willingly follow leaders who don't care for us!"

care (kâr) *v.* **1.** To be concerned or interested. 2. To provide needed assistance or watchful supervision.

HUMANS, for the most part, seem resistant to change. At times, even the best of us don't go willingly down the new path even when we know it is for our own good. We have confidence in the *old* ways. After all, they've worked for years, haven't they? (Or so we would like to believe!) So sometimes we need a push down the path by a leader who seems to know the way!

But, demanding high standards alone is only a small part of achieving high standards. Leadership involves, above all, the sacrificial effort on the part of the leader to nurture, to teach, to discipline, and to train subordinates in the elements necessary to accomplish their goals. Patton viewed the order to perform as only a starting point:

> *In carrying out a mission, the promulgation of the order represents not over ten percent of your responsibility. The remaining ninety percent consists in assuring by means of personal supervision on the ground, by yourself and your staff, proper and vigorous execution.*[1]

In other words, it's not enough just to tell them to do it! In **The One Minute Manager,** Kenneth Blanchard and Spencer Johnson advise us that there are five important steps in the teaching and training process. Besides just 1) telling them, we need to 2) show them, 3) let them try it, 4) observe and evaluate them, and then 5) tell them how they did.[2] It's a process that should be repeated as many times as necessary to accomplish the learning goal.

If Dr. Blanchard and Dr. Johnson are correct, it seems that teaching is one of the leader's most important jobs. Coach Joe Paterno agrees:

> *A coach, above all other duties, is a teacher. Coaches have the same obligation as all teachers, except that we may have more moral and life-shaping influence over our players than anyone else outside of their families. When a kid comes from a family that is not strong, our influence can become foremost.*[3]

Yet, Coach Paterno says that he wasn't always a good teacher. It's something he had to learn:

> *I was impatient with kids who didn't learn new plays now. If somebody had trouble mastering a physical technique, that was a little different, because I had always had trouble mastering techniques. But I never had any problem learning the mental part quickly, so I had no patience with anybody else who had trouble.*[4]

Clearly, teaching takes patience, a quality that lots of us as leaders don't naturally have; but if we don't *have* it, we need to *learn* it! If you don't have the patience to teach your team, they will assume that you don't care about them.

THEY MUST SEE THAT YOU CARE

To achieve long-term success, subordinates must believe in the goals of their organization, in their leaders, and in their own capability to accomplish their assigned objectives. True motivation comes from within, from their spirit, but the spirit that drives individuals and teams to superior performance seldom develops on its own. It is *inspired*—breathed in by motivating leaders. It never grows in teams run by leaders who do not demonstrate that they care about their teams. John Maxwell in his excellent little book, **Your Attitude: Key to Success**, reminds us, “People don't care how much you know until they know how much you care.”[5]

As did President Lincoln, Mr. Maxwell recognizes that humans are, first, emotional creatures. They must be won emotionally before they can be won rationally. They must see that you care about them.

Mike Shanahan, head coach of the Denver Broncos, summarized that thought in **Think Like a Champion**:

> *I know if somebody really cares about me and is really fighting for me, I'll go through a wall for them. The same works in reverse. If somebody knows you don't care about him and aren't really fighting for him, then he won't go through the wall for you.*[6]

CARING DOESN'T EQUATE TO SOFTNESS

Coach Shanahan knows that it's hard to get fired up for someone who really doesn't care about you. Notice also that Coach Shanahan didn't say that you have to like the coach to feel he cares for you. Andrew Hill wrote of Coach John Wooden (**Be Quick—But Don't Hurry!**), famed UCLA Bruins basketball coach, honored as "Coach of the Century":

> *During my years of playing for Coach, I can honestly say that many of the players didn't like him, though I never felt that he disliked us back. No doubt, he liked some more than others, but he wasn't one to socialize and schmooze. In fact, Coach later told me, "I don't think all of them ever liked me. But they're not going to like you when you make decisions that affect them." In many ways, I think that Coach also understood all too well that his job depended on the team's performance, not on how much the guys on the team liked him. He needed to be a firm disciplinarian, which is hardly the way to ingratiate yourself with a bunch of guys in college. He corrected, cajoled, and even yelled at times. I suspect that Coach suffered internally with the knowledge that kids were being hurt and lives were being altered, but he never changed his ways or his demeanor. Of course, the ultimate irony of this secret is that many years after graduating, there are countless players who never really liked Coach when they were playing for him but who now will tell you they love him.*[7]

Andrew Hill points out that, only in retrospect, are many of the players able to acknowledge Coach Wooden's caring. He had to be tough or he didn't really care about his team. Usually, players can sense the caring even when they don't want to admit it.

This raises an important point relative to the Blake/Mouton Managerial Grid®. If a leader cares deeply about production, but not much about people (9,1) does the leader truly care about production? We would answer with a resounding No! Who's going to get the job done? It's not the leader. Further, if a leader cares everything for people, but not much for production (1,9) does that leader truly care about people? Again, we must answer No! For, like Coach Wooden, if we don't demand high standards and push our people to achieve, they will not develop. We would be abrogating one of our most important leadership roles which is the responsibility to grow our people.

NOT A NEW CONCEPT

The power of demonstrated concern is not a new concept. Chang Yü, a contemporary of Sun Tzu, wrote:

> *When one treats people with benevolence, justice, and righteousness, and reposes confidence in them, the army will be united in mind and all will be happy to serve their leaders. The Book of Changes says: "In Happiness at overcoming difficulties, people forget the danger of death."*[8]

Chang Yü saw the bond between leaders and team members as indispensable in inspiring the team to attempt difficult objectives. Patton (in **War as I Knew It**) saw it from this perspective:

> *All officers, particularly General Officers, must be vitally interested in everything that interests the soldier. Usually you will gain a great deal of knowledge by being interested, but, even if you do not, the fact that you appear interested has a very high morale influence on the soldier.*[9]

And then there was that old softy, Melvin Zais, former commander of the 101st Airborne Division during the Viet Nam war:

> *You cannot expect a soldier to be a proud soldier if you humiliate him. You cannot expect him to be brave if you abuse and cow him. You cannot expect him to be strong if you break him. You cannot ask for respect and obedience and willingness to assault hot landing zones, hump back-breaking ridges, destroy dug-in emplacements if your soldier has not been treated with respect and dignity which fosters unit esprit and personal pride. The line*

between firmness and harshness, between strong leadership and bullying, between discipline and chicken, is a fine line. It is difficult to define, but those of us who are professionals, who have also accepted a career as a leader of men, ***MUST*** *find that line. It is because judgment and concern for people and human relations are involved in leadership that only men can lead, and not computers. I enjoin you to be ever alert to the pitfalls of too much authority. Beware that you do not fall into the category of the little man, with a little job, with a big head. In essence, be considerate, treat your subordinates right, and they will literally die for you.*[10]

WHAT ABOUT IN BUSINESS?

Now, some of you are sitting here reading and saying, "Sports, war? That's different. What about business?" Have you studied the story of Southwest Airlines under former CEO Herb Kelleher and President Colleen Barrett? Kelleher says, "We'd rather have a company bound by love than by fear." (The Southwest Airlines stock symbol is LUV.) But Southwest's performance record isn't a story of a squishy, fun-loving, but non-performing organization. They continue to win awards for on-time arrivals and departures, few instances of lost baggage, high customer satisfaction, and, above all, an excellent safety record.

Or consider what Robert Swiggett, former CEO of the Kollmorgen Company said about trust, caring, and a team-serving attitude:

The leader's role is to create a vision—not to kick somebody in the backside. The role of the leader is the servant's role. It's supporting his people, running interference for them, coming out with an atmosphere of understanding, and trust, and love. You want your people to feel they have complete control over their destiny at every level. Tyranny is not tolerated here. People who want to manage in the traditional sense are cast off by their peers like dandruff. We preach trust and the Golden Rule.[11]

It's not that Swiggett didn't know how to be tough, but he knew that demanding high standards alone wouldn't take his team to the performance level that he wanted. Team members need more than a paycheck to risk their devotions and energies. Concerned leadership is the lynchpin.

Unfortunately, one of the sobering thoughts in Swiggett's commentary is that, after years of leading and interacting with other American leaders, he believed tyrannical behavior to be a common, traditional form of management in the U.S. Our observations confirm his perception.

It seems to be a consistent theme among great leaders: they care for subordinates so much that a strong bond of affinity develops. As we will later learn, that is the basis of the strongest of the forms of organizational influence which is *personal power*. It is a manifestation of trust, and trust between leaders and their team members is what allows a team to grow beyond mediocrity, to the highest levels of performance.

THE BOTTOM LINE

So, what's the bottom line? If you don't care about the members of your team they will know within hours. There's no chance to build a foundation of trust on that relationship.

LEADING PRINCIPLE	When leaders demonstrate that they care about their subordinates, a strong bond of affinity develops. It is the platform upon which the strongest form of organizational influence—*personal power*—is constructed. It forms the basis of trust, without which a team cannot grow beyond mediocrity.

Chapter 22

USING POWER AND INFLUENCE

"We don't willingly follow leaders who misuse power!"

pow•er (pou'ər) *n.* **1.** The ability or capacity to act or perform effectively. **3.** Strength or force exerted or capable of being exerted; might… **4.** The ability or official capacity to exercise control; authority.

POWER is an elusive term, its substance difficult to define. So, in physics, rather than define its nature, physicists have chosen to define its effect which is the rate at which work is done. The magnitude of power for the physicist, then, depends upon how *much* work is done and how *fast* it is being accomplished.

In human terms, similar difficulties arise in determining what *power* is. Is it how many people are on our side? Is it how much information we have available? Is it the quality and quantity of skills that our team members bring to the game of work? Is it the intangible quality of charisma that leaders exercise? The answer is yes, all of those and probably dozens more.

If we revert to a definition similar to the physics description, we certainly can say, at the end of the day, whether a leader was powerful or not, simply by measuring how much work was done and how quickly it was accomplished. (We have already defined leadership as the process of accomplishing tasks by enlisting people and their talents to the work. The success of the leader in that endeavor certainly sheds light on whether he or she is powerful.) Looking, however, only at the end result does little to teach people what power is, how to acquire it, and how to use it. Further, it doesn't address whether a leader has acted in such a way that power can be sustained over a period of time.

Therefore, we really need to see what the leader was doing (and how and why he or she was doing it) in order to understand it. Only then does it become truly useful to us. Any useful study of power must identify the tools and techniques that successful leaders use to acquire influence with people. In other words, how does a leader enlist people to the cause?

TWO FORMS OF POWER

Leaders possess two fundamental forms of power: *pushing* power and *pulling* power. Pushing power, forcing someone to do something, is coercive, while pulling power is the power of persuasion. One drives while the other draws.

Both forms of power have legitimate uses, but they have dramatically different purposes and dramatically different effects when employed. Leaders who don't understand the difference often make a mess of things.

Pushing power is most useful for accomplishing rapid change, especially when the disposition of a team is resistive. Remember the tactics that Coach Norman Dale employed in the beginning of the movie **Hoosiers**? Or the methods of Brigadier General Frank Savage with the 918th Bomb Group in **Twelve O'Clock High**? Both teams were in need of tough, coercive leadership. They had little time in which to make meaningful changes, and they needed shock therapy for the purpose of redirection.

We do not want to give the impression that coercion is necessary for all situations in which team members are resistant. Obviously, most change engenders resistance because it represents something new and unfamiliar. A little bit of explanation and some education often do the trick, but teams sometimes become so entrenched in wrong habits that leaders have few options but to employ coercion. In situations where time is short, there may be no other options.

Pushing power, however, is limited in what it can accomplish. It is a great tool for turning a person or an organization, yet it never takes a team to Olympic-level performance. In other words, you can force change, but until you reform the thinking of the team, establishing new habits that make sense, you cannot sustain the change. The team will spring back to old habits as soon as you quit looking. So once a team is turned, pulling power must take over. Never forget that pushing power has the built-in disadvantage of increased mental resistance.

Pulling power, the power of persuasion, is the only way that high level performance can be achieved and sustained. Team members must want to achieve at high levels. They can't be forced. (Can you imagine trying to force an athlete to Olympic levels?) Do you remember Colonel Sihito's attempts to get Colonel Nicholson's British troops to build the **Bridge on the River Kwai**? He was unable to force them. Only when Colonel Nicholson won his demands and the British officers supervised the work did the bridge take shape. In the magazine Bits & Pieces (December, 1989), there is a wonderful adage: *You can hire people to work for you, but you must win their hearts to have them work with you!*

So which form of power is more important? It depends on the situation. Tu Mu, a colleague of Sun Tzu, advised:

> *If wise, a commander is able to recognize changing circumstances and to act expediently. If sincere, his men will have no doubt of the certainty of rewards and punishments. If humane, he loves mankind, sympathizes with others, and appreciates their industry and toil. If courageous, he gains victory by seizing opportunity without hesitation. If strict, his troops are disciplined because they are in awe of him and are afraid of punishment.*[1]

You need them both. You just need to know which one is appropriate for the situation that you're facing. (Isn't it terrible? Leaders are expected to read situations and know their people. Such a burden!)

CATEGORIZING SOURCES OF POWER

Pushing power and pulling power are commonly divided into five categories: 1) position power, 2) legitimate power, 3) referent power, 4) expertise power, and 5) personal power.

Position Power

Position power is the power of authority, rank, or, in the most primitive of cases, physical force. It is power that is vested in the position. The person who occupies the position wields the power. When used to offer rewards, it is a pulling force. When used to threaten or impose penalties, it is a pushing force. The statement that best characterizes the power of position is: "I'll do it because I know that you can make me (or that you can reward me in such a way that I find it difficult to refuse)." Sometimes, position power is called coercive power because that is the form that it most often takes.

Legitimate Power

Legitimate power is the power of tradition, values, laws, and duty. It is usually characterized as pushing power since laws, traditions, and values form the curbing of life. Organizational members perform tasks out of a sense of duty or conscience. The statement that best characterizes legitimate power is: "I'll do it because I've been taught that it's the right thing to do."

Peer pressure is a special form of legitimate power. It may be either constructive or destructive. Of course, in the mind of the one influenced, it is most often viewed as constructive.

Referent Power

Referent power represents the ability to influence as a result of one's reputation (or by virtue of the leader's association with other known leaders). Referent power may be either a pushing force or a pulling force. If a leader has a reputation for toughness, soon-to-be team members may begin to align themselves to the leader to avoid impending harshness. If a leader has a reputation for persuasiveness, potential team members are likely to align themselves to serve the new leader for the sake of approval. Therefore, referent power can also be a pulling force. The statement which best characterizes referent power is: “I'll do it because I've heard of you.” (Your skills, capabilities, demeanor, etc.)

Expertise Power

Expertise power is organizational power held by a leader as a result of the leader's known or proven knowledge and skills. It is almost always a pulling force. The statement that best characterizes the power of expertise to influence is: "I'll do it because I've seen what you can do." (I have faith in your skills.)

Tom Landry wrote:

> *A leader doesn't have to be the smartest member of a group, but he does need to demonstrate a mastery of his field. Mastery means more than just knowing information and facts; it requires an understanding of the information and the ability to apply that information. When I could tell my Giants' teammates how I knew ahead of time what the opposing offense would do on a given play, that knowledge gave me the authority I needed to establish my leadership.*[2]

Not only has Landry defined wisdom, he has also given great insight into one of the most important sources of influence—expertise power.

Personal Power

Personal power is power held by a leader as a result of the leader's personal influence over team members gained through interactions with the members. When a leader is trusted, respected, and loved, that leader usually has a large store of personal power with the team. The statement that best characterizes personal power is: "I'll do it because I trust and respect you."

ACQUIRING POWER

It's not enough to know the forms and categories of power; just as important are the methods by which the power is acquired. We have already stated that position power, for example, comes with rank. You don't have to work anymore for it once you occupy an organizational position. Reputation, of course, is acquired through past actions. Leaders who have done a good job (technically and with their team members on previous teams) usually have a good reputation. Look at the last two forms of power. Notice that expertise power and personal power both require personal (in person) interaction before any stores of power are built. Here's an important point: *If you don't spend time with your team members, you can't acquire the two strongest categories of pulling power*. Is it any wonder that leaders who spend all their time in meetings and in their offices are not well respected? You must be visible to lead successfully.

USING POWER

Leaders occupy an elevated position of influence and example. Therefore, they have a strong obligation to use their positions and influence wisely and justly. Robert E. Lee held his post in just such regard. He had a heightened sense of the sacred responsibility that leaders hold:

> *The forbearing use of power does not only form a touchstone, but the manner in which an individual enjoys certain advantages over others is a test of a true gentleman. The power which the strong have over the weak, the employer over the employed, the educated over the unlettered, the experienced over the confiding, even the clever over the silly—the forbearing or inoffensive use of all this power or authority, or a total abstinence from it when the case admits*

it, will show a gentleman in a plain light. The gentleman does not needlessly and unnecessarily remind an offender of a wrong he may have committed against him. He can not only forgive, he can forget; and he strives for that nobleness of self and mildness of character which impart sufficient strength to let the past be but the past. A true man of honor feels humbled himself when he cannot help humbling others.[3]

We, like Lee, should frequently be testing our motives as we lead. Are we in it for self-aggrandizement, or are we in it for the team?

Influence is an ever-changing commodity; it is not static, but dynamic. As already stated, sources of power are held in banks or stores in the mind of the person influenced. As such, a leader's power is likely to rise and wane over the course of his or her leadership tenure. Since leaders must keep the team's welfare ahead of individual team members, leaders will find themselves, at times, at odds with some. Lincoln said that you can fool all of the people some of the time, and some of the people all of the time, but you can't fool all of the people all of the time. The same goes for pleasing people. You will never please everyone all of the time. Get used to it.

ABUSING POWER

We have stated several times that leadership is, by its nature, an exercise in the use of power. Power can be used either for good or evil. Usually, when it is used to serve the team, it is being used appropriately; but when leaders use it to serve themselves, they are often abusing it.

Niccolo Machiavelli, in his classic work, **The Prince**, did not see it so. Instead, he viewed power as a tool to be garnered and used at any expense for the furtherance of the leader:

... [A] prince will never lack for legitimate excuses to explain away his breaches of faith. Modern history will furnish innumerable examples of this behavior, showing ... how the man succeeded best who knew best how to play the fox. But it is a necessary part of this nature that you must conceal it carefully; you must be a great liar and hypocrite. Men are so simple of mind, and so much dominated by their immediate needs, that a deceitful man will always find plenty who are ready to be deceived.[4]

In our view, leadership has a moral component. We don't agree with Machiavelli's dispassionate approach to the acquisition and use of power. Leadership is more than just getting people to do your bidding. If numbers of followers are the measure, then Adolf Hitler, Josef Stalin, and Mao Tse-Tung were great leaders. However, by most assessments (ours included), they all used their power for evil. They mercilessly murdered millions simply because of race or political disposition. The use of power in that manner, in our view, constitutes tyranny.

DISHONESTY: A BLATANT ABUSE

Perhaps the most common power abuse within business teams is dishonesty. When leaders purposefully mislead their team members, they do great harm, not just to their teams, but to the entire organization. Reputation is so hard to acquire, yet so easy to destroy. We heard of one chief executive recently who, when asked by an employee if the company was for sale, emphatically denied it. Within a few weeks, the company had been sold. The deal had been cut weeks earlier. The leader, of course, retired with a golden parachute. Employees within that company are understandably *very* bitter about being misled. The leaders who now suffer from that bitterness are the ones left to pick up the pieces. In the eyes of many of the remaining team members, the lies of one leader are evidence that *all* leaders in the company are dishonest. That's not fair or right, but it is reality.

Outright lies are not the only form of this type of power abuse. Dissembling is another. I'm sure you were taught by your parents that "a half truth is a whole lie." When leaders fudge their words with the clear intention of misleading, that's lying. If one must say, "It depends on what your definition of 'is' is," then one no longer has the best interests of the team at heart.

THE USE OF PHYSICAL FORCE

Physical force is the most primitive form of coercive power. Because it is so often abused, many people believe that all physical force is bad. Like it or not, however, civilization is based ultimately on the legitimate use of force. A small percentage of societal members tend to test the boundaries established by the society. They feel unbound by the legitimate power of the society. Unless there is consequence to the actions of these few, the legitimate boundaries of the society are eventually trampled and the society forced into disarray. Just as cattle push through an electric fence with no current, so does the "outlaw" segment of a society. Force, then, plays a necessary role in civilization.

In the hands of an abuser, force is a dangerous tool. As a result, checks and balances are necessary to offset the potential for power abuse. Noah Webster, famous American journalist and author of the first American dictionary, wrote:

> *Before a standing army can rule, the people must be disarmed; as they are in almost every kingdom in Europe. The supreme power in America cannot enforce unjust laws by the sword; because the whole body of the people are armed.*

Adolf Hitler knew that dispersed power was his enemy. He postulated: "The most foolish mistake we could possibly make would be to allow the subjected people to carry arms..." He proved his point in the Warsaw Ghetto in 1942.

The experiences of the Founders of our nation were riddled with the power abuses of European monarchs. As a result, they created a form of government in which power (including the ability to use physical force) is dispersed. Until recently, that principle has been a foundation stone of the Common Law of English-speaking peoples.

As English moral and political philosopher Thomas Hobbes wrote:

> *A Covenant not to defend myself from force, by force, is always void. For... no man can transfer or lay down his Right to save himself from Death.*

Fortunately, in the context of the civilizations of our businesses, force seldom needs to be used. Most employees live within the societal boundaries. Checks and balances of power exist in the form of policies, levels of leaders, and even in the form of employee unions. Yet, many businesses still must establish security forces to protect the employees and the business assets, usually from outside threats. It is evident that organizations and societies cannot long exist without leaders who understand power and exercise it appropriately.

THE BOTTOM LINE

So, what's the bottom line? Leadership is an exercise in the acquisition and wise use of power. Use it with forbearance and care, always remembering Lord Acton's admonition: "Power corrupts. Absolute power corrupts absolutely."

LEADING PRINCIPLE

Power is a measure of a leader's ability to influence the members of a team toward accomplishment of a goal. It is the currency of leadership; and, like money, it is neither good nor evil. It is a commodity that may be used for proper purposes or improper ends. Wise leaders accumulate power in all of its forms and learn to select the proper form to address each problem. Like a master carpenter, a wise leader has a toolbox full of tools and the ability to employ each for its intended purpose.

"Do not be afraid of any man, regardless of his size.
In time of need, just call on me and I will equalize."

(Samuel Colt)

Chapter 23

NAVIGATING THE CORPORATE TERRAIN

"We don't willingly follow leaders who are poor route finders!"

nav•i•gate (năv'ĭ-gāt) *v.* **1.** To plan, record, and control the course and position of (a ship or aircraft). **2.** To follow a planned course on, across, or through: *navigate a stream…*

goal (gōl) *n.* **1.** The purpose toward which effort is directed; an objective… **2.** The finish line of a race.

ROUTE-FINDING—determining the paths to intermediate and final objectives—is one of the most important jobs of the leader. I remember a platoon sergeant who, during a military field exercise, demonstrated a disturbing inability to find objectives using map and compass. His squad leaders quietly took over those functions, assigning knowledgeable squad members to perform the navigation chores. Nevertheless, the platoon sergeant was thoroughly discredited in front of his soldiers. He had lost their trust and it was never regained.

The Selway-Bitteroot Wilderness in Central Idaho is the largest wilderness area in the lower forty-eight states. A vast expanse of roadless mountains, timber, rivers, and streams, it is, even to the initiated, a formidable obstacle to travel. Home to the Salmon River, the famed "River of No Return" (named by Lewis and Clark on their westward journey to the Pacific), its mountains, canyons, cliffs, and talus slopes sometimes seem an endless tract of sameness.

Navigating through this wilderness, even with the aid of global positioning system (GPS), can be daunting. Constant fixing of position is necessary to avoid disorientation, even during full daylight. Quit paying attention to your topographical map and compass, and you can soon find yourself in the bottom of the wrong drainage. Even if you know where you are, getting to the next objective may, at times, seem next to impossible. Enveloped in a blanket of steep terrain, up, down, and around is the usual order of march.

Sounds a lot like your job, right? Actually, navigating the Bitteroot and directing the activities of an organization are not so dissimilar as you might think. Both require an end goal, a starting point, a direction of march, intermediate objectives, and methods for negotiating obstacles. Plus the recognition that there are a whole bunch of people on this march with you.

THE END GOAL

As we learned earlier in this study, the leader must be able to envision the team mission, where the team needs to go. Further, the leader must have a clear (though ever-changing) picture of the team's potential and the intermediate goals necessary to accomplish the mission. If the person steering the ship cannot envision the destination, the outcome will be in doubt!

Where does a leader acquire such vision? Usually it's from past experience. They've been there before. William F. ("Buffalo Bill") Cody began guiding Westward-bound wagon trains out of Weston, Missouri, at the age of 14. He didn't just decide to do it. He accompanied other trips first. He had been there, so he had a picture of the end destination and a proven route to get there.

Hard work has a lot to do with it, too. Vince Lombardi knew more about football than most other coaches of his era because he studied football in greater detail than other coaches. Similarly, Admiral Hyman Rickover became the guru of nuclear power, not because he was smarter than everybody else, but because he worked harder at understanding it. That understanding created clear pictures of the potential for using nuclear energy in powering warships.

In business, it's not much different. Experience is a necessary component of great leadership. It's a lot easier to get there again if you've been there before, but wise leaders also recognize that vision is necessary for *all* of the team members. Keeping people in the dark is a prescription for slow, inefficient progress. People who are kept in the dark are not confident to take the next step on their own. They also become irritable and resistant to leaders who keep them in such a state. Smart leaders keep their team members well informed and solicit their input on direction, intermediate goals, and methods for overcoming the obstacles which are an inevitable part of every journey.

Patton admonished his leaders to tell people what to do, but not to tell them how to do it. He had found that subordinates have good ideas. He had learned that wise leaders involve their team in studying problems and fashioning solutions. The outcome is often far more expedient than what the leader would have devised alone.

Finally, great leaders also recognize that there really isn't one final objective. Teams are never done. They must always progress. There is always a new horizon, a new mountain to climb, and another river to cross.

A STARTING POINT

With the end goal identified, leaders need to verify the team's starting point. In vector analysis, there are three parts to a vector: a starting point, a direction, and a magnitude. Even if you travel in the right direction for the right distance, unless you know where you are starting from, you're not going to end up where you think you ought to be.

How can you find your location? How do you know where you are? In GPS navigation, several satellites identify your location from different orbital positions. By comparing the results of each satellite channel, GPS can accurately locate you to within a few meters. It's a process called *triangulation*.

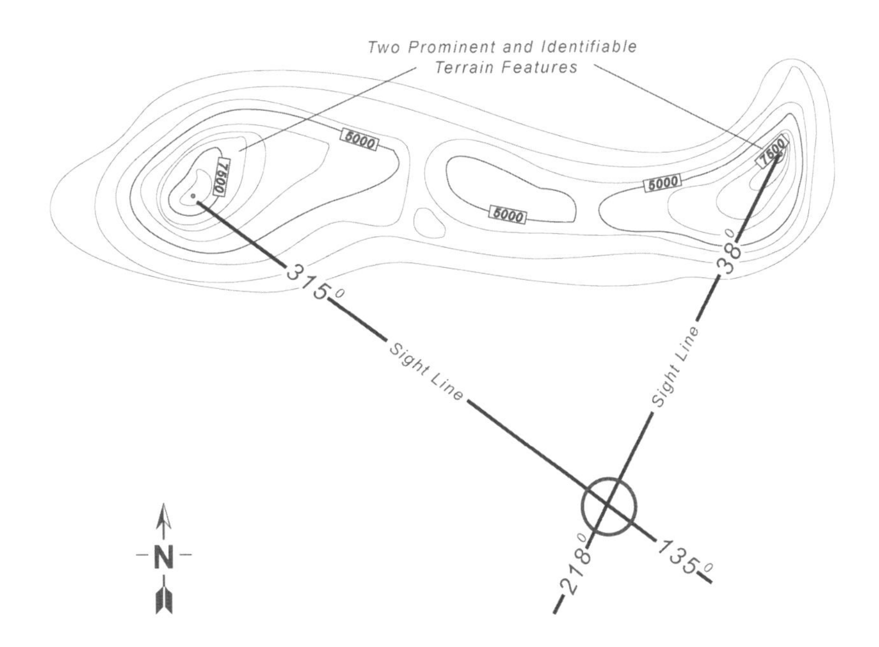

Figure 23-1 Triangulation

Without GPS, you can use a topographical map and compass to accomplish the same task. Orient the map toward north using the compass. (Your compass must be adjusted to compensate for the difference between true north and magnetic north, a difference known as *magnetic declination angle*, since the earth's magnetic poles do not correspond precisely with it's axial poles. The higher north in latitude, the greater the difference between true north and magnetic north for most locations.) Next, find two distinctly recognizable points within your range of vision and identify them on the map. (Sometimes not such an easy task!) With your compass, determine the direction (or *azimuth*) to each point. Finally, from each of these two map points, plot a *back azimuth* (accomplished by adding or subtracting 180 degrees to the azimuths that you first measured). The lines will intersect and, if you've done your work correctly, the convergence of the two lines is your position. (See Figure 23-1, Triangulation.)

In both processes, multiple perspectives were necessary to find your position—your starting point. There's an important lesson here for all of us in business: *A single perspective is usually insufficient for solving a complex problem!* To find out where my company is, I need to ask my team members and my customers. Further, I need to engage (and teach my team to engage) in a daily process of self-assessment to keep tabs on my location. Not only does that help me with a starting point, but it also helps me to make mid-course corrections.

Coach Tom Landry recognized this early in his coaching career. He instilled a culture of self-criticism within his teams for the purpose of constant improvement:

> *Perhaps the biggest factor in the Cowboys' reputation as strong finishers was our quality control program. When I first hired a coach for the sole purpose of studying our films and analyzing our own performance, we waited till the end of the year to evaluate which plays we ran well, which required fine-tuning, and what things needed to be thrown out or forgotten altogether. But I quickly concluded, "Why wait until after the season when it's too late to improve this year?" That's when we began evaluating the effectiveness of all areas of the team every four or five games.*[2]

A ROUTE OF MARCH

Once you know your location, you can plot a course to the final objective—a route of march. Plotting a course in advance of starting the trip gives everyone on the team a picture of what is ahead. It also affords an opportunity to consider the obstacles the team is likely to encounter during the march. (And, obviously, a chance for the team to plan how the obstacles will be overcome.)

We would like to emphasize again how important it is for leaders to involve their team members in plotting the route. Clear pictures of the destination, likely obstacles, and the next step in the route are what allow team members to move with efficiency and wisdom. Too often, leaders formulate pictures of where they want their teams to go but never share that picture with their teams. Then they are upset when the team blunders or ends up in the wrong location. "Stonewall" Jackson often fell prey to that mistake. His strategies were, for the most part, born of simple genius, but his attitude toward his subordinate leaders and team members was that they didn't need to know much; they only needed to execute his orders. As a result, his cavalry and artillery were often not well positioned to exploit the initial successes of the main body.

INTERMEDIATE OBJECTIVES

In the Bitteroot country, if you must navigate for more than a few miles, it's unlikely that you'll be able to see your final objective. There's too much forested, mountainous terrain. So, if you can't see to the end, how can you get there?

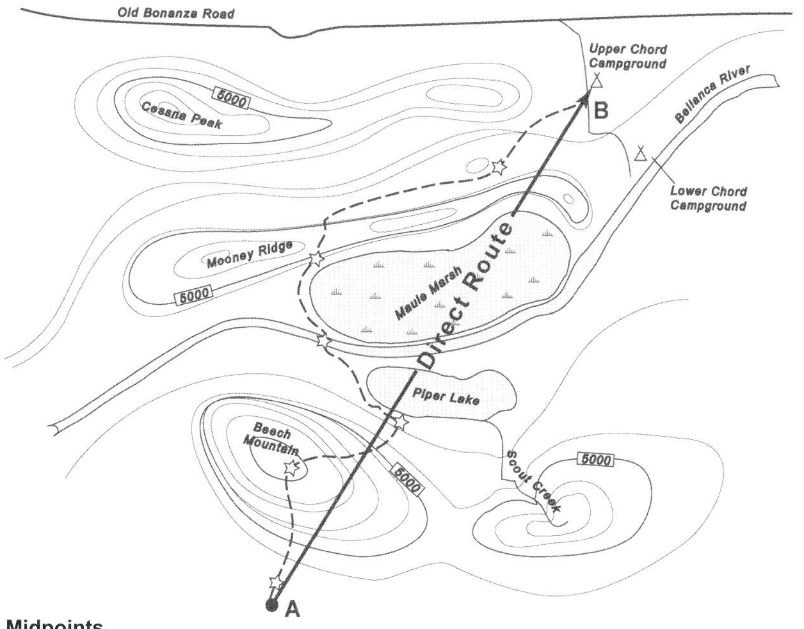

Figure 23-2 Tactical Midpoints

Intermediate objectives are the answer—*tactical midpoints* along a predetermined course. (See Figure 23-2.) For example, to navigate a 10 mile overland route through the Bitteroot country, the destination wouldn't be visible at the start. Plus, in between, there would be a lot of difficult terrain. If, however, we knew the starting point and the destination, from the map we could determine the overall direction of march from our map. By dividing the march into pieces, the end is attainable.

Here's the process: Open up the compass (which, again, has been adjusted for magnetic declination angle). Point the compass along the azimuth that you need to travel in order to reach the final objective. Find a prominent point (rock, tree, etc.) along that path that you will be able to keep in sight. Close up the compass and navigate to that point. Now do it again. And again. If your measurements are accurate, you will eventually reach the final objective.

This example provides some important lessons for leaders in goal-setting. People have a hard time going to places they can't see or imagine. That's why one of the leader's most important jobs is to present a picture of the destination. But sometimes the final destination is so hard to envision, leaders have to establish closer destinations—objectives that are easier to see—so that team members can navigate in the right direction and see their progress toward the goal.

DON'T SET THE OBJECTIVES TOO FAR APART

Not only must objectives be visible, they must also be, and appear, achievable. (You can see from one side of the Grand Canyon to the other. That doesn't mean you can step across it.) If team members don't think goals are attainable, they won't attack them with conviction. Just like training a horse to jump, if you start the bar too high, the horse learns to balk rather than to jump. So, you start the bar low enough that the horse can succeed. As the horse's skill and confidence increase, you raise the bar.

Similarly, as you establish intermediate objectives for your team, you must consider the skill level of the team. If they are just learning, the intermediate objectives will probably need to be closer together and more easily achievable.

OVERCOMING OBSTACLES

Just because you can see the objective doesn't mean that it's going to be a straight-line route of march to get there. The path is almost always strewn with obstacles that you must negotiate such as streams, rocks, or dense forest. So, though you start out on a heading toward the final destination, you may need to change direction (detour) to get around obstacles.

A couple of points about obstacles. First, if you don't expect them, you are likely to be overwhelmed when you face them. Think through obstacles before you encounter them.

Second, when you're negotiating obstacles, your attention can't be elsewhere. You must be focused on the immediate task. You shouldn't be looking toward the next objective.

Third, when you have overcome an obstacle, it's important to get your bearings again and to get your eyes back on the objective that you're trying to achieve. Stop and look where you're going.

Finally, no matter how hard you look for a way around an obstacle, there may not be one. Sometimes you just have to stop and cross the river.

LOGISTICAL SUPPORT

Sometimes people (and businesses) set out on journeys for which they are ill-equipped. If you don't have the resources to navigate and overcome obstacles, you are going to be disappointed in the results and your team members are going to lose a lot of confidence in you as a leader. That's one of the reasons that it is so important to plan the route well and engage your team members in analyzing the route and the obstacles before you start.

IF YOU GET LOST

Even during the best-planned journeys, you can become temporarily disoriented. Overcoming obstacles, especially ones that you didn't anticipate, can create fatigue and confusion. It is precisely at those times that your leadership is most needed, because there is a tendency for the team to start in the wrong direction.

People who become disoriented in the wilderness tend to wander panic-stricken and aimlessly. Without training, it's hard to stay calm. Even the experienced feel the sense of fear that arises in these difficult situations. So what do the survival experts tell us? Stay put. Don't move just for the sake of moving. It wastes energy and increases confusion. The same goes for the corporate situation. Companies in crisis tend to panic just like people. They feel that they must do *something* when, in fact, doing nothing for the moment may be the best solution. You need a chance to calm down, evaluate the situation, and develop a plan. Remember, most situations are neither as good or as bad as they first seem. You usually have time to plan a response.

KNOWING WHEN YOU'RE THERE!

We've already stated that there is seldom a single, final objective. Leaders must always be looking toward the next goal, but you must also recognize that, when you get to the objective you originally planned, it is valuable to stop, mark the occasion, recognize the accomplishment, review progress, and then plan for the next move. It is disheartening for team members to work hard at achieving an objective, only to receive no recognition for their efforts.

One more point on knowing when you're there. Sometimes, when you get there, it doesn't look like what you thought it would! (Remember Spencer Tracy as Major Rogers in **Northwest Passage** as his Rangers arrived at Ft. Wentworth?) A desirable quality of leaders is the ability to withstand disillusionment. It's important for you, and probably more important, for the sake of your team. Find the good in the objective you just accomplished and learn from it.

DEFINING SUCCESS

Goal-accomplishment is inextricably tied to the definition of success. The way you view it has a lot to do with knowing when you're there. Coach Mike Krzyzewski of the Duke Blue Devils dispensed wise advice on this subject:

When most people think of success, they think of the season ahead and they set a final destination goal. In my line of work, many coaches select winning the national championship as their end goal. But I think that's a pretty shallow view of success—because only one team can win it all. So if everyone chose that definition of success, then nearly everybody would have an unsuccessful year. I'm also certain that many people out there set that goal because fans and the media tell us that winning the national championship is the only way we'll be successful. Well, if you're always striving to achieve a success that's defined by someone else, I think you'll always be frustrated...[3]

THE BOTTOM LINE

So, what's the bottom line? Get your team members involved in determining the tactical midpoints. You'll be surprised and gratified by their ingenuity.

LEADING PRINCIPLE

Leading a corporate team along a business path is a lot like navigating in the wilderness. You need to know where you want to go, where you are, and what intermediate objectives you need to reach in order to achieve your end destination. Route-finding becomes easier when team members participate in determining the intermediate objectives and remain constantly aware of direction and current location.

Chapter 24

DISCIPLINING THE TEAM

"We don't willingly follow leaders who don't understand the meaning of discipline!"

dis•ci•pline (dĭs'ə-plĭn) *n.* **1.** Training expected to produce a specific character or pattern of behavior, esp. training that produces moral or mental improvement. **2.** Controlled behavior... **3a.** Control obtained by enforcing compliance or order. **b.** A systematic method to obtain obedience. **c.** Order based on submission to authority. **4.** Punishment to correct or train. **5.** A set of rules or methods...

team (tēm) *n.* **1.** *Sports & Games* A group on the same side. **2.** A group organized to work together. **3a.** Two or more draft animals...

DISCIPLINE is one of the most misunderstood expressions in the English language. Gather a hundred Americans in a room, give them one word in which to define discipline, and ninety of them will say *punishment*.

Yet the root meaning of discipline is at least as closely related to *instruction* as it is to punishment. Discipline has been described as "training that develops self-control, character, or orderliness and efficiency." The word *discipline* comes from the Latin root *disciplina*, meaning teaching or learning. *Disciplina* comes from the Latin noun *disciplus*, meaning student or pupil. Interestingly, the root definition, *instruction*, is listed as obsolete in some English dictionaries (a most damning commentary on the American understanding of the process of discipline). Penalties are certainly part of the discipline process, but teaching and training are more closely aligned with the root meaning.

PURPOSES OF DISCIPLINE

What purpose does discipline serve? In 1838, Antoine Henri Jomini (renowned Swiss military strategist and philosopher) observed the value of discipline in this way:

> *Concert in action makes strength; order produces this concert, and discipline insures order; and without discipline and order no success is possible.*[1]

Jomini knew that team effort directed toward a common goal is the engine of success. Strength comes from the orchestrated actions of individuals harnessed together, pulling toward a unifying objective.

Harnessed together and pulling in the same direction. That's a useful image of what a team is and does. In fact, a review of the definitions of *team* in **The American Heritage Dictionary** provides a graphic mental impression: "two or more draft animals."

Why two or more animals? To multiply power! In a two-horse hitch, neither horse alone can accomplish what both together can achieve (assuming, of course, that they have been trained to pull together). It is through their *combined* effort—the multiplication of individual strengths in concert—that great tasks are accomplished. That's what **synergism** is: t*he action of two or more substances, organs, or organisms to achieve an effect of which each is individually incapable.*[2]

Human teams are no different. They're just more complex. And, considering the phenomenal capability of the human brain, they have astonishing potential for accomplishment.

Notice, however, that just harnessing team members together isn't enough to makc a good team. If you have ever attended team horse pulling contests at the state fair, you know that it isn't always the biggest team that wins. It's the team that pulls at the same time, in the same direction—the team whose combined effort creates the most force at the right time.

That's where discipline comes in. By training individual team members *how* and *why* to pull together a concert of force is created.

Hence, the primary purpose of discipline is to forge the raw material of individual team members (the building blocks of a team) into an implement far more powerful than any single member.

THE DISCIPLINE CYCLE

Forging individuals into teams requires constant communication of a special type called performance feedback. We need to know how we are doing with respect to standards and expectations. When we don't meet them, we need to know. When we exceed them, we need to know.

Figure 24-1 (The Discipline Cycle) illustrates a cycle of performance with which most of us are familiar. It shows an expected range of performance, sometimes a little better than the norm and sometimes a little worse. When performance drops below the expected range, however, leaders need to calibrate their team members, providing correction or even reprimand to draw performance back into line. Similarly, when team members exceed the expected range of performance, leaders should encourage and praise the performance, making it clear that the noted behavior is worthy and desirable. When performance is particularly noteworthy, reward may be in order. *Reward* is usually associated with giving something to someone, perhaps time off, money, promotion, etc. It should be reserved for exceptional performance. At the other end of the spectrum is a process called punishment. *Punishment* is usually associated with taking something from someone, such as pay, position, or opportunities. Punishment usually has a special condition: it is normally

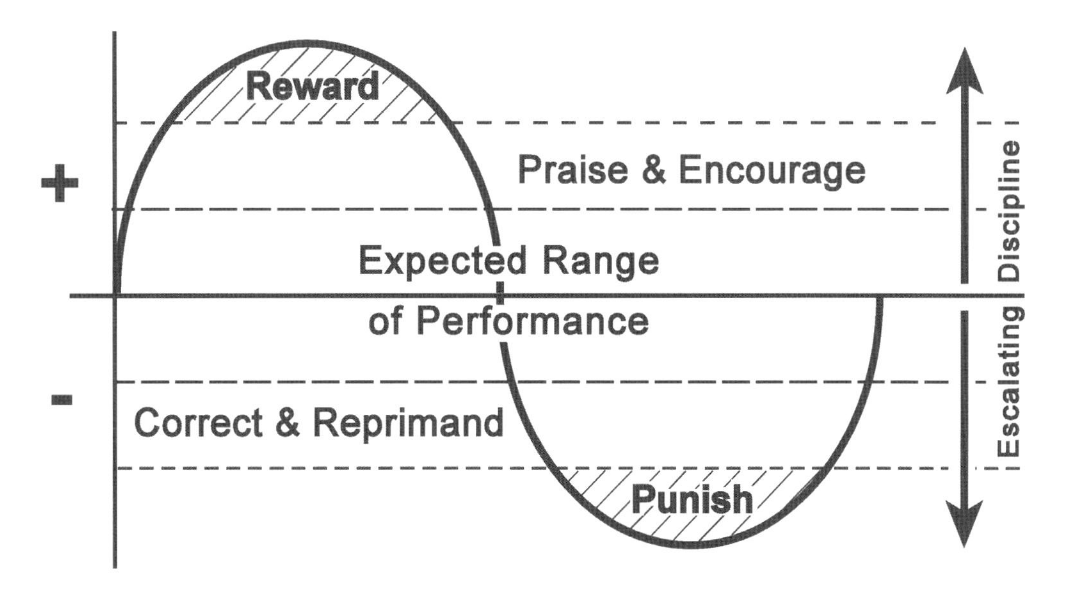

Figure 24-1 The Discipline Cycle

associated with a violation of known rules. It is designed to address an attitude of, "Yah, I know what the rules are, and I ain't playin' !"

Contrary to what most Americans think, praise is an important part of the discipline process. Patton wrote:

> *Remember that praise is more valuable than blame... Officers who fail to correct errors or to praise excellence are valueless in peace and dangerous misfits in war.*[3]

So the process of escalating discipline shouldn't just proceed in the negative direction. It should also progress through encouragement and praise all the way to reward for exceptional performance.

CREATING A DISCIPLINED TEAM

In a broad sense, then, discipline goes beyond adjusting undesirable behavior through reprimand and punishment. Far more, it is the process of instructing, training, encouraging, persuading, exhorting, praising, reprimanding, and sometimes punishing those over whom we have authority (and for whom we bear responsibility) toward individual and team development for the purpose of accomplishing a mission.

Sounds a lot like what good leaders are supposed to do, doesn't it? Build effective teams and orchestrate their actions to achieve objectives? Building, however, always occurs in stages. In construction, it is a metamorphosis from planning to site preparation to utility installation to laying a foundation and so on until finish work is completed. The end result is the product of a planned, sequentially executed process. (And then the upkeep begins!)

So it is in the building of human teams. They're constructed in phases starting with determination of mission (based on need), creation of an organizational structure (the human implement that will facilitate mission accomplishment), selection of team members suitable to fill the structure, development of individual skills, advancement toward team skills, and maturation into that magic state called teamwork which is when it all begins to click.

The tools and the techniques that you use to build a team depend, in great part, upon where you are in the building process. Less mature teams and team members usually need more direction. They may not know how to play their positions or even the game. They may not even understand what a team is. That means you're going to spend more of your time on fundamentals and philosophy than on tactics and strategy. Anyone who has coached a little kids' soccer team, for example, knows that you can't orchestrate the actions of players who don't yet possess fundamental skills, but, like it or not, working through each phase is part of building a disciplined team. Get used to it, Coach!

TEACHING VALUES

The magic of *team* is difficult, if not impossible, to achieve without a foundation of strong values. Indeed, team *thinking* is itself a value. Therefore, in creating disciplined teams, great coaches don't confine their efforts only to the areas of knowledge and skills. Rather, their instruction permeates to the core of individual team members. Coach Joe Paterno said it well:

> *The job of a teacher of academic subjects is to implant facts, ideas, and ways of thinking, and so expand kids' minds. In teaching excellence in football, we have to reach the soul of a player. Football is played, above all, with the heart and mind. It's played with the body only secondarily. A coach's first duty is to coach minds. If he doesn't succeed at that, his team will not reach its potential. Therefore, at the heart of our curriculum, as important as skills and tactics, are the purposeful uses of emotion, commitment, discipline, loyalty, and pride. In facing the realities of competition, a person learns the meaning of excellence and professionalism. Not only to an athlete but to any person, that makes a decisive difference in how he feels about himself.*[4]

Yet values are hard to teach for leaders who do not live them. "Do as I say, not as I do" leaders have scant credibility. And without credibility, a leader has little influence beyond coercion. Don't underestimate the power of leading by example!

THE LEADER'S ATTITUDE

Instruction, training, persuasion, exhortation, praise, reprimand, and punishment are all tools available to the leader for the development of team members and a disciplined team. To a great extent, the effectiveness of these tools depends upon the attitude of the one who uses them. Good leaders (whether praising, reprimanding, or simply instructing) approach their team members with the purpose of individual and team improvement; they know that course correction or reinforcement rendered in the right spirit is far more likely to be accepted and utilized. On the other hand, correction and instruction delivered with the motive of self-exaltation is apt to cause the recipient to abhor the leader.

Sixteen years after the battle of Gettysburg, Major General John M. Schofield (one of Grant's western theater commanders during the American Civil War) cautioned the cadets at West Point against egotistical and abusive discipline:

> *The discipline which makes the soldiers of a free country reliable in battle is not to be gained by harsh or tyrannical treatment. On the contrary, such treatment is far more likely to destroy than to make an army. It is possible to impart instruction and to give commands in such a manner and such a tone of voice to inspire in the soldier no feeling but an intense desire to obey, while the opposite manner and tone of voice cannot fail to excite strong resentment and a desire to disobey. The one mode or the other of dealing with subordinates springs from a corresponding spirit in the breast of the commander. He who feels the respect which is due to others cannot fail to inspire in them regard for himself, while he who feels, and hence manifests disrespect toward others, especially his inferiors, cannot fail to inspire hatred against himself.*

General Schofield's experience taught him that the "desire to obey" comes from leaders exercising power in a respectful way (including the imposition of reprimand and punishment when necessary). Conversely, he learned that "strong resentment" was the likely outcome of egotistical abuse of position and authority. Schofield's advice has been memorized (though not always practiced!) for decades by every member of the United States Corps of Cadets.

THE BOTTOM LINE

So, what's the bottom line? Do you "feel and, hence, manifest" the respect which is due to others? Or have you bought into the bankrupt philosophy that "they have to respect me because I'm their boss?" Are your subordinates and your children disloyal and disrespectful toward you? Do they resent you as a leader? Are they in need of "discipline"? Maybe it's time that you found out what the word "discipline" really means.

LEADING PRINCIPLE Discipline is the process of instructing, training, encouraging, persuading, exhorting, praising, reprimanding, and sometimes punishing those over whom we have authority (and for whom we bear responsibility) toward individual and team development for the purpose of accomplishing a mission. The primary purpose of discipline is to forge the raw material of individual team members into an implement more powerful than any single team member.

"Whoever loves discipline loves knowledge,
But he who hates reproof is stupid."

(Proverbs 12:1)

Chapter 25

ENCOURAGING CRITICISM

"We don't willingly follow leaders who don't tell us how we are doing!"

crit•i•cize (krĭt' ĭ-sīz') *v.* **1.** To find fault with... **2.** To judge the merits and faults of; analyze and evaluate.

NOTHING (nor anyone) improves without analysis and criticism, yet, no one likes to be criticized for deficient behavior or performance. We tend to respond with outward anger if we think we can get by with it, or passive resistance if we think we can't. Until a person (or a team) can accept and profit from criticism, a sure sign of maturity, the player (or the team) cannot grow.

Since leaders are supposed to constantly improve their teams, it seems logical that they should teach team members how to embrace, employ, and provide critical comments including positive comments. Unfortunately, many leaders unwittingly do just the opposite, and they criticize in a manner that unnecessarily alienates their team, creating a barrier to performance improvement which is difficult to overcome.

CONSTRUCTIVE OR DESTRUCTIVE?

Criticism can either be *constructive* or *destructive*. Though sometimes outwardly similar, they are dramatically different from the perspective of intent. In constructive criticism, the motive is to improve a person or an organization. In destructive criticism the motive is self-aggrandizement. The first is designed ultimately to build up. The second is designed to tear down.

Tearing down is easy. Building up is hard. Sam Rayburn, famed Speaker of the House of Representatives, was fond of saying, "Any jackass can kick down a barn, but it takes a good carpenter to build one."

A jackass or a carpenter? One of our favorite poems asks the question, **Which Are You?**

I watched them tearing a building down,
A gang of men in a busy town;
With a ho-heave-ho and a lusty yell
They swung a beam and the sidewalk fell.
I asked the foreman, "Are these men skilled,
And the men you'd hire if you had to build?"
He gave a laugh and said, "No indeed!
Just common labor is all I need.
I can easily wreck in a day or two
What builders have taken a year to do!"

And I thought to myself as I went my way,
Which of these roles have I tried to play?
Am I a builder who works with care,
Measuring life by the rule and square?
Am I shaping my deeds to a well-made plan,
Patiently doing the best I can?
Or am I a wrecker, who walks the town,
Content with the labor of tearing down?

Constructive criticism may also tear down in the beginning. As in body-building, constructing muscle requires that it first be *de*constructed by working against resistance in a controlled process. With proper rest and nutrition, however, the muscles are restored to a level stronger than the original one.

Sometimes criticism is like that. It hurts at first. It may even create a sense of fear in the one criticized, especially coming from a tough leader like Bobby Knight or Bill Parcells or Hyman Rickover or George Patton. If the leader's motive, however, is to make a better player, and not to self-aggrandize, then the criticism, if well founded, is probably sound.

A caution is in order here. Sometimes it's hard for leaders to separate what's good for the player versus what builds their own egos. Perhaps the best antidote against ego-driven criticism is to ask ourselves these questions: "Why am I saying this? What is my motivation? Is it to make me look better, or is it to improve the team?"

GIVING CRITICISM

The purpose of criticism should always be to build up and to improve a person, a process, or a team. (We do not deny, however, that there are some for whom criticism is not effective. They have not been acting in good faith and are not committed to the team. They are *outlaws* within the organization and must be ejected.)

Having the right motive doesn't mean that criticizing will be pleasant. Most of us are conflict-avoiders. We hesitate to criticize because we don't like disagreeable conversations, though we say it's because we don't want to hurt someone.

Certainly confrontation should not normally be sought, especially with team members who have been acting in good faith, but we soon learn that, to lead, we must face into conflict. To evade it is an abrogation of duty, a disservice to the team member and, ultimately, to the team.

Coach Pat Riley, author of **The Winner Within** and extraordinary architect of professional basketball teams, equates refusal to face conflict with character failure in the leader: "Avoiding the solution of a tough, miserable, volatile problem is not discretion. It is cowardice." [1]

So the question is not *whether* criticism is necessary, but *how* to deliver it. *Respectfully* is the answer. We can bear tough messages if they are delivered with respect, if we know that the boss, though clearly angry, really cares about the team. Humans are malleable. As we learned earlier, they can adapt to many styles, soft or tough, as long as they know that their leader is honest and concerned ultimately for their well-being, but they don't perform for (nor do they accept criticism from) those for whom they have little respect.

Of course, there's another variable at play here which is the personality of the one criticized. Tough criticism may work for one person and not another. If you have children, you have learned that they need different discipline. One may be verbally sensitive, correcting behavior instantly. Overly tough criticism may break this one's spirit. For the other, a nearby grenade detonation may be necessary! As we learned in the chapter on "Consistency", Coach Joe Paterno said that understanding the difference between the two types of players is at the heart of coaching.

Perhaps the best rule for determining how much force to use is *just enough to get the job done*. Here's a good rule: Are you criticizing in a way that your players can respect? They may not like the criticism, but they need to respect you.

RECEIVING CRITICISM

To criticize objectively and without arrogance is desirable; to accept honest criticism graciously, though it be distasteful, is venerable. He is a mature individual who thoughtfully receives criticism and objectively considers it before responding. King Solomon cautioned his children: “Reprove a wise man, and he will love you.” (**Proverbs** 9:8.)

Sometimes we are eager to render criticism, yet reluctant (or even incensed) to receive it. Yet if presented with a pure motive—for the purpose of improvement—criticism usually deserves consideration.

One problem, of course, is the way in which the criticism is presented. Every parent knows that a child who comes with tender heart, asking about the rigidity of a new family rule, is far more likely to receive a favorable audience than one who arrives with the pronouncement, "This is stupid!" Again, the method of message delivery is at least as important as the message.

Another problem is ego. "How dare she question my decision!" says the boss. Yet, if the criticism is honest, relevant, and tastefully delivered (not in a fashion of rebelliousness), it should be accepted with graciousness.

Herein lies the crux of *questioning attitud*e, something that Rickover forever preached to his progeny. The proper questioning attitude inquires of the decision or direction. It does not, except in rare circumstances, challenge the authority structure, the foundation of a civilized organization.

The purpose of the question is to ensure that all pertinent data have been considered before action is taken. Clearly, it is a skill critical to team problem solving; therefore, it should be taught to and demanded from every team member.

RESPONDING TO CRITICISM

Early in the movie, **Hoosiers**, Coach Dale was talking to Cletus, the principal, about George, the interim coach. George had a high opinion of his own coaching abilities and was threatened by the arrival of Coach Dale. In fact, he had engaged in degrading Coach Dale to some of the town's citizens. Cletus told Coach Dale: "Oh, don't worry about George. He'll be right with ya when ya start winnin'."

What a sad commentary on people! They tend to withhold support from their leaders until they start winning. Unfortunately, leaders need support *before* they start winning. It makes winning easier!

But if you're in the leadership business, you'd better get used to it. It's an old human trait. Niccolò Machiavelli in **The Prince** wrote:

> *There's nothing more difficult to plan, more doubtful of success, nor more dangerous to manage than the creation of a new system. For the initiator has the enmity of all who would profit by the preservation of the old system and merely lukewarm defenders in those who would gain by the new one.*

In leading, criticism comes with the territory. How leaders respond to it says a lot about their maturity. Tom Landry wrote:

> *...[A] crucial test for any leader is how he handles criticism. Everyone makes mistakes. But when a leader makes one, people almost always notice and criticize him for it. As a football coach, the crowd boos when the play you called fails; the commentators in the broadcast booth question your thinking... Sometimes a good leader has to be able to listen to criticism and change his plan accordingly. Other times he's better off just ignoring the critics. The trick is in deciding which to do when. That often means considering the source. Some of my critics I paid attention to because I knew them to be thoughtful, knowledgeable people who took the time to try to understand my position before they criticized it. Others I found easy to ignore because they had no idea what they were talking about. Perhaps the most important step in dealing with criticism is realizing it's part of the job.*[2]

Perhaps no one in modern times has better demonstrated how to respond to criticism than Abraham Lincoln. Few have been criticized as often or as venomously as Lincoln. The criticism cut deeply for he took it to heart; and criticism, especially from his "friends," was particularly hurtful. Yet his humble attitude always carried the day.

Once, his Secretary of War (and former political rival), Edwin Stanton, called Lincoln a "damned fool" when speaking to a Congressman. When the event was reported to Lincoln, he responded to the effect that: "If Stanton said I was a damned fool, then I must be, for he is nearly always right."[3] In one stroke, Lincoln showed himself to be wise and emotionally controlled, while, at the same time, casting Stanton in the role of fool.

IGNORING CRITICISM

We should appreciate the criticism of those who are laboring with us. Usually, it's presented in a spirit of helpfulness, but sometimes criticism is gratuitous and unworthy of consideration. You've got to consider the source. President Lincoln said:

> *If I were to read, much less answer, all the attacks made on me, this shop might as well be closed for any other business. I do the very best I know how, the very best I can, and I mean to keep doing so until the end. If the end brings me out all right, what is said against me won't amount to anything. If the end brings me out wrong, then angels swearing I was right would make no difference.*

Finally, it's easy to criticize and hard to produce. President Theodore Roosevelt recognized this when he wrote:

> *It is not the critic who counts; not the one who points out how the strong man stumbled, or how the doer of deeds could have done them better. The credit belongs to the man who is actually in the arena; whose face is marred with dust and sweat and blood; who strives valiantly; who errs and comes short again and again; who knows the great enthusiasms, the great devotions, and spends himself in a worthy cause; who, if he wins, knows the triumphs of high achievement; and who, if he fails, at least fails while daring greatly; so that his place shall never be with those cold and timid souls who know neither victory nor defeat.*

THE BOTTOM LINE

So, what's the bottom line? The difference between valuable criticism and useless fault-finding is the motive from which it is rendered. If provided for the sake of improvement, it can be a powerful performance enhancer. If delivered with the purpose of degradation, it is usually not worth listening to. Discerning which motive unveils the character of the critic.

LEADING PRINCIPLE

No one (nor any team) improves without constructive criticism. All good coaches know that they must observe, evaluate, and provide feedback to their players if they expect the team to make positive changes. Yet, few people enjoy being criticized. Therefore, successful leaders learn to provide criticism in a way that's "hearable." Further, good leaders teach players how to coach one another and to provide constructive feedback to their coaches as well.

"A fool rejects his father's discipline,
But he who regards reproof is prudent."

(Proverbs 15:5)

Building Trustworthy Teams

- A Team Approach
- Ingredients of a Team
- Steps in Building a Team
- Characteristics of Good Team Members
- The Team Feeling

Great accomplishments are nearly always the result of teamwork. Consequently, to be effective, leaders must be team-forgers, assembling the components of a team and molding them into synergistic units capable of accomplishing far more than the sum of uncoordinated individual efforts.

Chapter 26

A Team Approach

"We don't willingly follow leaders who don't foster teamwork!"

team•work (tēm'wûrk') *n.* Cooperative effort by the members of a group or team to achieve a common goal.

THOUGH a simple word, teamwork is a complex concept. Many leaders seem plagued with a naive belief that a group of people gathered together to perform a task constitutes a team. But, as the definition indicates, a team is far more than just the right number of people with the right skills.

Admiral Rickover wrote:

> *Operating nuclear plants safely requires adherence to a total concept wherein all functional elements which support operations are recognized as important and each is constantly reinforced. Even after each support function—technical, training, quality assurance, radiological control, maintenance, etc.—is adequately staffed and trained, they must be effectively integrated if they are to support sound operating decisions.*[1]

Integration is the difference. Bill Walsh, legendary head coach of the San Francisco '49ers and, more recently, the head coach of the Stanford University Cardinals football team has stated:

> *The real task in sports is to bring together groups of people to accomplish something... Those teams that have been most successful are the ones that have demonstrated the greatest commitment to their people. They are the ones that have created the greatest sense of belonging. And they are the ones that have done the most in-house to develop their people.*[2]

Coach Walsh told us that it is not enough to develop excellent knowledge and skills. We must also create a sense of belonging—a sense that is only developed by coaches who take a personal interest in cultivating the team through the improvement of the team members.

WHY CREATE A TEAM?

There are at least three major reasons for creating a team. Teams can accomplish more than individuals acting alone, teams can usually solve problems better than individuals, and teams offer mutual encouragement to their members.

Greater Accomplishments

The ability of teams to accomplish more than individuals acting alone results from much more than sheer numerical strength. Teams of people, when properly integrated provide strength through diversity of knowledge and skills, diversity of life experiences, and differing perspectives and viewpoints. The team *fabric* that is created, if woven by a skilled leader, can be stronger than if made of homogeneous threads.

Diversity lends strength by allowing members of the team to see problems and obstacles from different viewpoints. An obstacle which seems insurmountable from one team member's perspective may have already been overcome by another. This leads to mutual encouragement and elevated confidence in the team's capabilities.

Mutual Encouragement

The members of teams are individually complex and different. Seldom are all team members simultaneously thinking and performing at their peak capabilities. Yet, sports and industrial history are both rife with inspiring stories of teams that pulled together under adverse circumstances to accomplish almost unbelievable feats.

Mutual encouragement is fundamental to that process. The desire and ability of team members to raise the expectations and spirits of their colleagues is a vital factor in accomplishing difficult tasks. It is clear that one of the leader's greatest tasks is to orchestrate the attitudes and efforts of the members of the team and to cultivate an environment of mutual support.

Better Problem-Solving Capabilities

Teams are often much better equipped through diversity and numbers to solve problems than individuals alone. Properly selected and properly led teams can efficiently study problems, develop alternatives, and propose recommendations.

Problem-solving teams need not be afflicted by the inefficiencies so commonly attributed to committees. The Toyota Motor Company has demonstrated the value of studying problems down to the lowest affected levels through quality circles. The success of Ford's Taurus program was based on diverse problem-solving groups. Problems can be solved rapidly when a team has the requisite technical knowledge, clear objectives, and a competent leader who encourages open communication.

CULTIVATING THE TEAM

The commitment to build a team should not be made lightly. It is expensive in time for both team members and leaders, in financial resources, and in emotional dedication. It cannot be done in a sterile, uninvolved manner. It demands team leaders and team members willing to subordinate their own personalities and desires to create the team environment. It does not mean that team members sacrifice their principles. The best teams are those whose members work closely together while maintaining a sense of personal responsibility and accountability for the outcome.

Team building is accomplished most effectively by solving problems together. Nothing draws a group of people together more completely than facing and resolving difficult issues. As already discussed, team building requires a worthy, unifying cause; talented, committed people; demanding, caring leaders; a directed program of training, practice, and player development; and time, dedication, and persistence.

Continuous training is critical. Just as for sports, training in industry should be a never-ending process. No team ever gets good enough that it doesn't need practice. The skills that served so well yesterday are dulled without practice. Constant evaluation and improvement are hallmarks of a vibrant team.

It is clear that good coaches cost a premium. The planning, execution, team coaching, and individual counseling necessary to effect good training only occur when a team has a good coach. The practice of drawing trainers (and leaders) from the ranks of those who can't get along with others or who have shown that they cannot perform adequately is exceptionally short-sighted and destructive to an organization. The best members of operating teams who also show a penchant for teaching and demonstrate a positive team attitude are the best candidates for training (and leadership) positions. The team structure must be built in a way that desirable candidates have incentives to serve in coaching positions. The loss of shift differentials, overtime pay, or other monetary benefits must be offset at least with prospects of better future work opportunities. Without incentives, candidates with the requisite skills and knowledge will often not be inclined to become coaches.

TIME, DEDICATION, AND PERSISTENCE

The process of cultivating a team is time consuming and frustrating. Sometimes it seems that progress is more often lost than advanced. But experienced leaders recognize that the most lasting changes in organizations take time, dedication, and persistence to plan and implement. General Creighton Abrams once admonished his staff that elephants can only be eaten one bite at a time. President Eisenhower similarly expressed the sentiment:

> *The older I get the more wisdom I find in the ancient rule of taking first things first—a process that often reduces the most complex human problems to manageable proportion.*[3]

Leaders must expect setbacks and frustrations. If you know that they will occur, they aren't so hard to accept when they happen.

THE BOTTOM LINE

So, what's the bottom line? A team is far more than a conglomerate of skilled players. Without adept leaders, teams are unlikely to rise above mediocrity in performance.

LEADING PRINCIPLE	Great accomplishments are nearly always the result of a team approach. Consequently, to be effective, leaders must be team-forgers, assembling the components of a team and molding them into synergistic units capable of accomplishing far more than the sum of uncoordinated individual efforts.

Chapter 27

Ingredients Of A Team

"We don't willingly follow leaders who don't understand the ingredients of a team!"

in•gre•di•ent (ĭn-grē'dē-ənt) *n.* An element in a mixture or compound; a constituent.

How, then, does one forge a team? Are talented leaders and skilled team members enough? Or are there other important components? The ingredients of successful team development vary little, whether in business, sports, or combat. Besides leaders and team members, teams need mission, team structure, resources, a communications network, rules of play, a training regimen, and a means to evaluate player and team performance.

MISSION

A legitimate, well-stated mission is essential for transmitting the team vision and setting the team direction. All subordinate team goals should support the team mission.

Failure to establish the team mission in the minds of all of the team members is a serious, but common problem. Team members need the focus and direction that a well-conceived mission provides.

TALENTED PLAYERS

Talented players result from properly established player selection criteria followed by appropriate initial and continuing training. All three areas are sometimes slighted, but *continuing* training is probably the most often neglected.

It's important to have good players; but the best individual players aren't always the best team players. Team synergy can often overcome talent deficiencies. Good coaches know the value of developing *team consciousness* as well as developing individuals to their peak potential.

TOOLS AND EQUIPMENT

Proper tools, equipment, and other material resources are essential to team success. Though good teams can often excel without top-of-the-line resources, there is a point at which talent cannot overcome resource deficiencies.

Successful team leaders assess the tools of competing teams and adopt those that they can use. Good coaches avoid the *not-invented-here* syndrome.

RULES OF PLAY

As Coach Landry advised us, games cannot be played or even enjoyed if the rules are not well-established. Nothing is more frustrating or confusing than a set of rules which is continuously changing. Over time, the rules and standards certainly must change as a game matures, but the rule changes must enhance the game. Most often, they should evolve only as necessity dictates.

It is incumbent upon leaders to stay abreast of the rules and ensure that their players clearly understand them. That is a difficult task in the industrial arena, especially regarding the rules of hazardous waste and environmental protection. The best protection is to enlist the aid of experts to educate team members and then reinforce the knowledge through self-assessment.

TEAM STRUCTURE

Proper team structure organizes players in a way that uses their talents most effectively. Team structure also defines for players their relationships, the chain of authority within the team, and the lines of communication to coordinate their efforts with one another and with the team leader.

Inefficient structure is analogous to poor design. Regardless of execution by talented players, poor team structure will lead to errors.

COMMUNICATIONS NETWORK

A clear, open communications network is fundamental to fluid teamwork. Successful teams are bathed in a process of constant, open, evaluative communication. Players and coaches all feel confident to express their ideas and object to actions or plans which they believe are not in the team's best interest. If sports teams of just a few players rely so heavily upon communications, how much more should business teams with many players and a complex mission?

CONVENTIONS OF PLAYER INTERACTION

Every team must have a culture defined by written and unwritten conventions of player interaction. These conventions help to delineate player roles and interrelationships. In many ways, they define the personality of the team. They form an important part of the discipline which helps to glue the team together.

A team without such a personality or culture lacks identity. Players may have difficulty subordinating personal goals to team goals in that circumstance.

Similarly, every business has such a set of conventions that help to form a culture. The difficulty is in ensuring that the culture changes to reflect changes in risk.

TRAINING AND PRACTICE

A directed program of training, practice, and player development is essential for any team to excel. We would not even consider fielding a serious sports team without such a program. Yet, business teams often do not receive the same level of training and practice as sports and military teams. When we consider the potential consequences of industrial failure, neglect of individual and team training is unreasonable.

Industrial team training should include a structured program for administering controlled facility casualty and emergency drills. The drills should be conducted frequently enough to provide practice and opportunity to assess team performance.

SELF-ASSESSMENT

A continuous self-assessment, analysis, and feedback process is necessary to improve individual players and the team as a whole. Healthy self-assessment involves both players and coaches. It thrives within the open environment of communications.

Self-assessment is poorly conducted by many teams because some players and coaches haven't learned that criticism can be positive. Coaches often use criticism for personal ego-building and players take offense. Such interactions result in petty arguments rather than team improvement.

For self-assessment to be effective coaches must teach players by personal example to subordinate ego. The sacrifice of short-term personal goals can be overcome by the value and personal satisfaction in building a successful team.

TALENTED LEADERS

In many ways, the success of a team relies upon talented, competent, caring leadership. Teams with the best players often fail when poorly coached. The leader gives meaning to the mission, direction by example, and motivation through coaching. All other team elements can be in place, but without this catalyst, the team will degrade.

The question is often asked, "Where do I find such leaders?" The answer is that good leaders are cultivated by serving under other good leaders. They pick up their styles, their habits, their deportment, and their values. On the other hand, poor leaders learn their trade in the same way. Every leader, then, has the job of cultivating subordinates into leaders for the future.

THE BOTTOM LINE

So, what's the bottom line? Just having the right number of team members with the right skill does not make it a team. Talented leaders are necessary to organize and orchestrate the efforts of the players.

LEADING PRINCIPLE Besides leaders and team members, teams need a clear mission, an efficient team structure, open lines of communication, reasonable rules of play, an effective and continuous training regimen, and a means to evaluate player and team performance.

Chapter 28

STEPS IN BUILDING A TEAM

"We don't willingly follow leaders who don't know the steps in team building!"

build (bĭld) *v.* **1**. To form by combining materials or parts; construct. **3.** To develop or give form to according to a plan or process; create: *build a nation.*

NOTHING is more influential in pulling a team together than a talented coach. Whether leading in sports or in industry, great leaders learn to pilot a team consistently to success in the best and worst situations. Without competent leaders, no strategy can succeed.

Learning to lead is a lifelong experience. Fortunately, the lessons of leadership are neither mysterious nor obscure. The characteristics of leadership are written in the pages of history for any who are willing to study it. Great leaders are distinguished by shared traits, skills, and principles which may be analyzed and learned. What, then, must good leaders do?

MASTER THE GAME CONCEPT

Successful coaches have a superior understanding of the game in which they are involved. They understand the purpose of the game, its rules, and the skills necessary for players to perform well. Industrial leaders are no different. They must know the technology of their businesses, the boundaries which define them, and the skills necessary for successful industrial teams.

ENVISION THE TEAM MISSION

The leader must be able to envision the team mission, the team's potential, and the intermediate goals necessary to accomplish the mission. If the leader has no vision of the future, the team has little chance of success. Great leaders also recognize that the best visions and the best ideas may come from the team members themselves. As a result, they encourage team members to stretch their own visions for the future.

ESTABLISH THE TEAM STRUCTURE

Leaders understand that poorly structured teams are inefficient teams, so they clearly establish the structure, the lines of authority, and the lines of communication for the team. Team leaders recognize that well-conceived and well-defined structure is an aid rather than a hindrance to open communications and participative management.

COMMUNICATE THE TEAM MISSION

Envisioning team potential and the mission of the team is insufficient for success. Great coaches know that they must recreate in the minds of the players the vision that they themselves have. Leaders must communicate the team mission, the team potential, and the team goals clearly and unmistakably.

INSPIRE A TEAM ATTITUDE

Successful leaders recognize the importance of a positive, enthusiastic, team attitude. They also understand that the leader is the source of that attitude. Unenthusiastic leaders create unenthusiastic subordinates. Leaders have a special responsibility to speak and act in encouraging ways even when they don't feel like doing so.

DEFINE THE ROLES OF THE PLAYERS

Great leaders use their vision and experience to clearly define the roles of each team member. They wisely discern individual players' potential, and how each player can best be employed to assist the team. Leaders also encourage team members to expand their own roles and take on new responsibilities.

SET THE STANDARDS OF PERFORMANCE

Leaders set the standards of performance, not only through stating the standards, but also through living the standards. Team members need distinct role models who demonstrate the quality levels to which tasks are to be performed.

CREATE AN OPEN COMMUNICATION ENVIRONMENT

Good coaches understand the value of responsive, thinking team members, and therefore, create an environment that values honest, evaluative communication among subordinates. They encourage constructive criticism at all levels.

DEVELOP A TRAINING PROGRAM

Successful leaders are the result of successful subordinates. Great coaches recognize that success comes through training, practice, and player development. Therefore, at the heart of their programs is a structured program of teaching, training, and practice.

DEMONSTRATE A CONCERNED, CARING ATTITUDE

Demanding high standards of player performance is only half of the equation for success. The other half is the leader's demonstration of a concerned, caring attitude. People serve leaders, not causes. Team leaders must also serve players if truly high standards are to be achieved and maintained.

GARNER SUFFICIENT RESOURCES

True leaders know that a team must have the right resources to succeed. Good leaders do their best to acquire the resources necessary to achieve, but great leaders know that the most important of all resources is the composite of players on the team. As a result, leaders invest much time and effort in developing the individual players.

COACH INDIVIDUALS AS WELL AS TEAMS

Great leaders recognize differences in people and work with them as individuals as well as teams. Coach Joe Paterno tells us that good coaches learn that everybody is different:

> *Eventually, through trail and error, I found out there are different ways to handle different people. So I began to be a coach.*[1]

One great dichotomy of leadership is that successful leaders must, on one hand, be consistent in their treatment of the members of a team, and, on the other hand, coach each team member in a way that maximizes that member's potential. Not until Coach Paterno recognized that need, he says, did he begin to be a coach.

LEAD BY EXAMPLE

Great organizations are not built by "Do as I say, not as I do" leaders. Good leaders model the values that they espouse. They understand the incalculable effect of leading by example on team building and team performance.

RECOGNIZE AND RESPOND TO CHANGE

The best leaders recognize new and changing circumstances and initiate team changes to meet new situations. They don't wait to get run over by the train. Yet, they do not bend where principle is involved, even in the face of adversity.

TEACH SUBORDINATES THE MEANING OF WINNING

Great leaders are also great teachers. One of the most important lessons they teach their teams is the definition of winning. They know that winning is not winning every game but winning games consistently over a long period of time. They also know that winning is the result of every team member and the team itself living up to its potential.

EMPOWER SUBORDINATES

One of the hardest tasks of a leader is trusting subordinates to perform after they have been given a task. Patton said it was one of the most difficult leadership lessons he ever learned. There is a lot of talk about empowerment in many industrial organizations today, but empowerment is predicated upon trust and training. Trust is not evident in many organizations as we study the divisions between leaders and subordinates or management and labor. Trust is based upon honesty.

There can be no empowerment without training. An attempt to build empowered teams is doomed to failure unless it is based on a rigorous training program in which team members prove their ability to perform.

PROVIDE CONSTRUCTIVE EVALUATION

The best coaches provide constant, constructive evaluation of individual and team performance. They encourage all members of the team, whether leaders or subordinates, to similarly evaluate individual and team performance.

REDIRECT, RETRAIN, AND RETRY THE TEAM

Finally, good leaders redirect, retrain, and retry their teams until they reach their potential. They tune the team like an engine and continuously look for ways to improve it.

THE BOTTOM LINE

So, what's the bottom line? Here's a visual synopsis of the steps leaders must take to build a team and accomplish a mission. (See Figure 28-1, The Ten P's of Project Management.)

LEADING PRINCIPLE

Learning to lead is a lifelong experience. Fortunately, the lessons of leadership are neither mysterious nor obscure. The characteristics of great leaders are written in the pages of history for any who are willing to study it. Great leaders are distinguished by shared traits, skills, and principles which may be analyzed and learned.

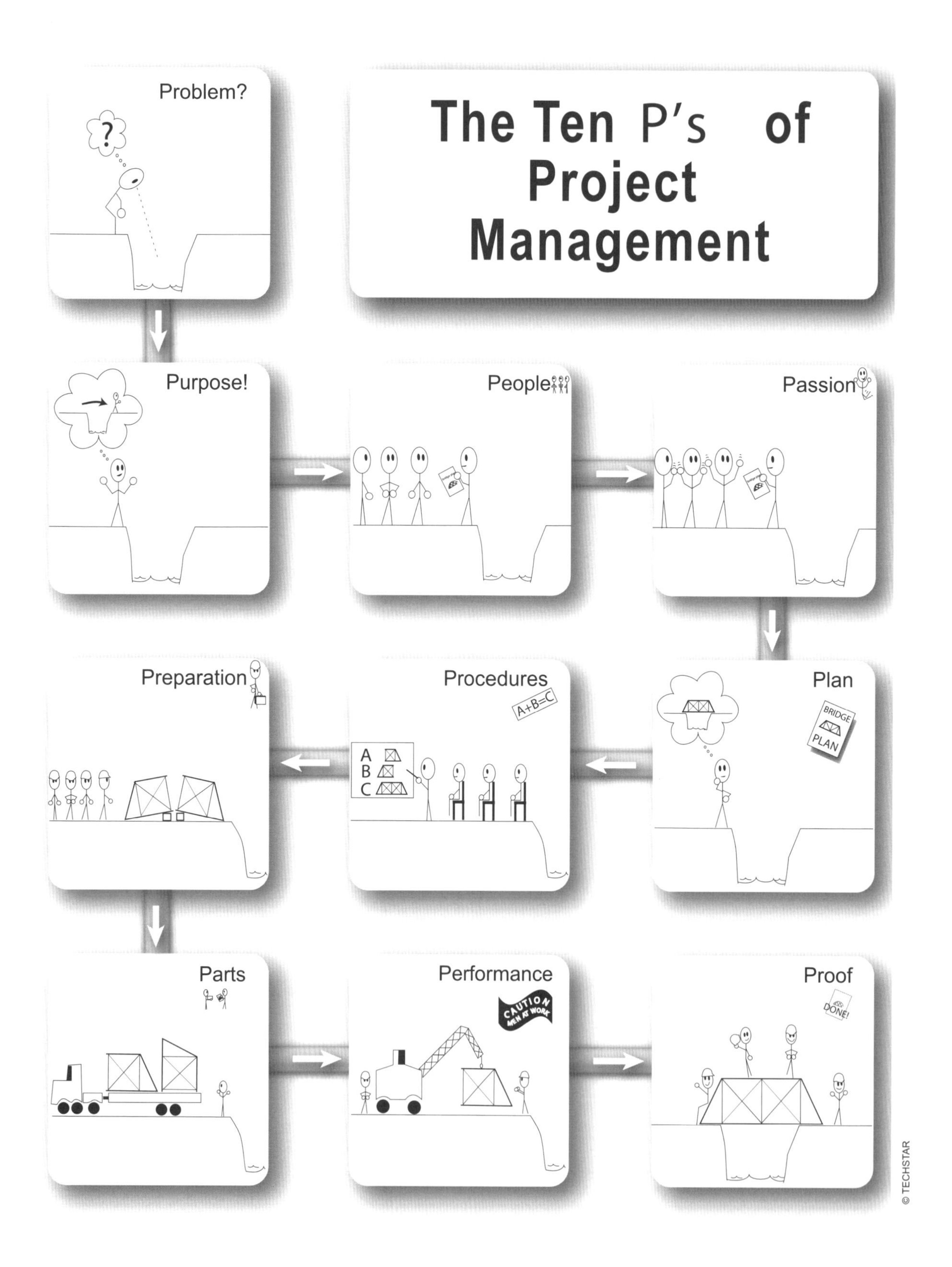

Figure 28-1 The Ten P's of Project Management

Chapter 29

Characteristics Of Good Team Members

"We don't willingly follow leaders when we have a rebellious attitude!"

teach•a•ble (tē'chə-bəl) *adj.* **2**. Able and willing to learn.

EVEN the best leaders can't teach anything to players who are unwilling to learn. Coach Joe Paterno said it this way:

> *I said in those days that to have a great team you've got to have we and us people. We won't have a great team unless you as an individual work at making this squad a team. At making so deep a total commitment to every guy who wants to win that he puts aside any thoughts of personal glory. Everything for the team. Don't look for what you're going to get, but for what you're going to contribute. Praise each other. Help each other. Be interested in each other. Learn what makes the other guy tick. Don't grandstand, because grandstanding only causes resentment. Don't sulk and pout and shoot your mouth off. All that does is alienate your teammates. Don't boast. Have confidence that you're the best—but don't talk about it.*[1]

ADOPT A TEACHABLE ATTITUDE

A teachable attitude is one of the most important characteristics of a team player. A team member cannot learn without first committing to learn.

ACCEPT THE AUTHORITY OF THE COACH

Committed team players accept the authority of the coach even when they don't like the coach. Certainly there are circumstances in which a team member, out of principle, must refuse to participate on a team, but personalities must, to the extent possible, be subjugated to the process of building a team.

COMMIT TO BUILD THE TEAM

Team players are loyal to the cause, the leader, and the team. They commit to the struggle to make a team and are willing to sacrifice for the sake of the cause and the team.

PRACTICE DILIGENTLY

Good team members are not just "game players". They give their best effort during practice when there is no crowd to cheer as well as during the game.

COMMUNICATE HONESTLY

Successful team members communicate honestly with the coach and their teammates. They recognize the value and need of open communication in team building and problem-solving.

LISTEN TO CRITICISM

Team players learn to listen to criticism, evaluate their own performances, and adjust their behavior accordingly. They also develop the skill of rendering constructive criticism in a manner that does not obscure the message. They know how to provide constructive criticism to their bosses as well as their colleagues.

THE BOTTOM LINE

So, what's the bottom line? Trustworthy team members are as important to building good teams as are trustworthy leaders. You don't have to like the coach to play for the coach.

LEADING PRINCIPLE	Even the best leaders can't teach anything to team members who are unwilling to learn. A teachable attitude is a vital characteristic of a team player.

Chapter 30

The Team Feeling

"We don't willingly follow leaders who don't engender a feeling of esprit within the team!"

esprit de corps [ĕ-sprē'] (də kôr') *n.* A common spirit of comradeship, enthusiasm, and devotion to a cause among the members of a group.

ALMOST everyone has been on a winning team at some time. The team feeling is one of camaraderie at overcoming difficulties and a feeling of pride in the team itself. The French called it *esprit de corps*—the spirit of the unit or body.

The team feeling is created by many elements. Among them are well-defined goals, challenging work, a caring leader, a role model leader, and successful performance.

WELL-DEFINED GOALS

A common objective pulls teams together. When team goals are well-defined, team members can pull together and the team feeling is enhanced.

CHALLENGING WORK

Teams need challenging work and high performance standards. Low standards lead to complacent attitudes and careless performance.

A CONCERNED, CARING LEADER

There is little that creates the team feeling more than a leader who not only sets high standards of performance, but also demonstrates commitment to the team and to the players through individual coaching and counseling. A team must have good players but it is unlikely to win consistently without a good coach.

A LEADER WHO SERVES AS A ROLE MODEL

Leaders who live up to the standards that they set are invaluable in creating the team feeling. Little is more destructive to the morale of teams than leaders who demand more of the team than they themselves are willing to give. A leader who serves as a role model is a part of the team. A leader who doesn't will be effective only in proportion to the amount of coercive power that they are able to wield.

SUCCESS ON THE FIELD OF PLAY

Success—realizing that all the hard work has paid off—is an important factor in developing the team feeling. When a team learns how to win and what it feels like to win, winning becomes easier. Players begin to realize that the team can accomplish more working together in a concerted effort than any one member and more than all the players working independently. Players who have learned that the essence of teamwork is helping one another and relying on one another never forget the value of a team.

THE BOTTOM LINE

So, what's the bottom line? Winning truly is its own reward. The feeling of *esprit* that belonging to a high performance team engenders creates for most an unforgettable feeling.

LEADING PRINCIPLE When a team learns how to win and what it feels like to win, winning becomes easier. Team members begin to realize that the team can accomplish more working together than all the players working independently.

Conclusion

IN February, 1860, Abraham Lincoln opened an address to those gathered at the Cooper Institute in New York City in this manner:

> *The facts with which I shall deal this evening are mainly old and familiar; nor is there anything new in the general use I shall make of them. If there shall be any novelty, it will be in the mode of presenting the facts, and the inferences and observations following them.*[1]

As Mr. Lincoln felt then, so we now feel. We have presented no new ideas in **Trustworthy Leaders**—only old and longstanding principles discovered and rediscovered by countless generations faced with the task of organizing teams and orchestrating their efforts to solve complex problems. If there is value in this work, it is in providing new perspective on old ideas, creating better images of the way leaders should lead.

The theme has been that effective leadership is founded upon trust, "a firm reliance on the integrity, ability, or character" of a leader. Though coercion is a legitimate and necessary tool for some circumstances, it doesn't engender much trust and it is very limited in what it can accomplish. Olympic-level achievements are never the result of coercion. Such accomplishments result only from *want-to* motivation, an impelling force usually instilled by a trusted coach, teacher, or mentor.

Just reading a book cannot impart the knowledge and skills necessary to effectively lead. Instead, learning to lead is a life-long endeavor, never finished, always a work in progress. We wish to encourage you toward continued study of this most important of skills through reading literature, viewing films about leading, and observing both good and bad leaders in you life. *Helpful Books* and *Helpful Films* are abbreviated bibliographies that we have included at the end of this book to assist you in your study.

We hope that we have re-awakened your interest in learning about leading.
Best wishes for a productive journey!

APPENDIX A

TECHSTAR Personality Types

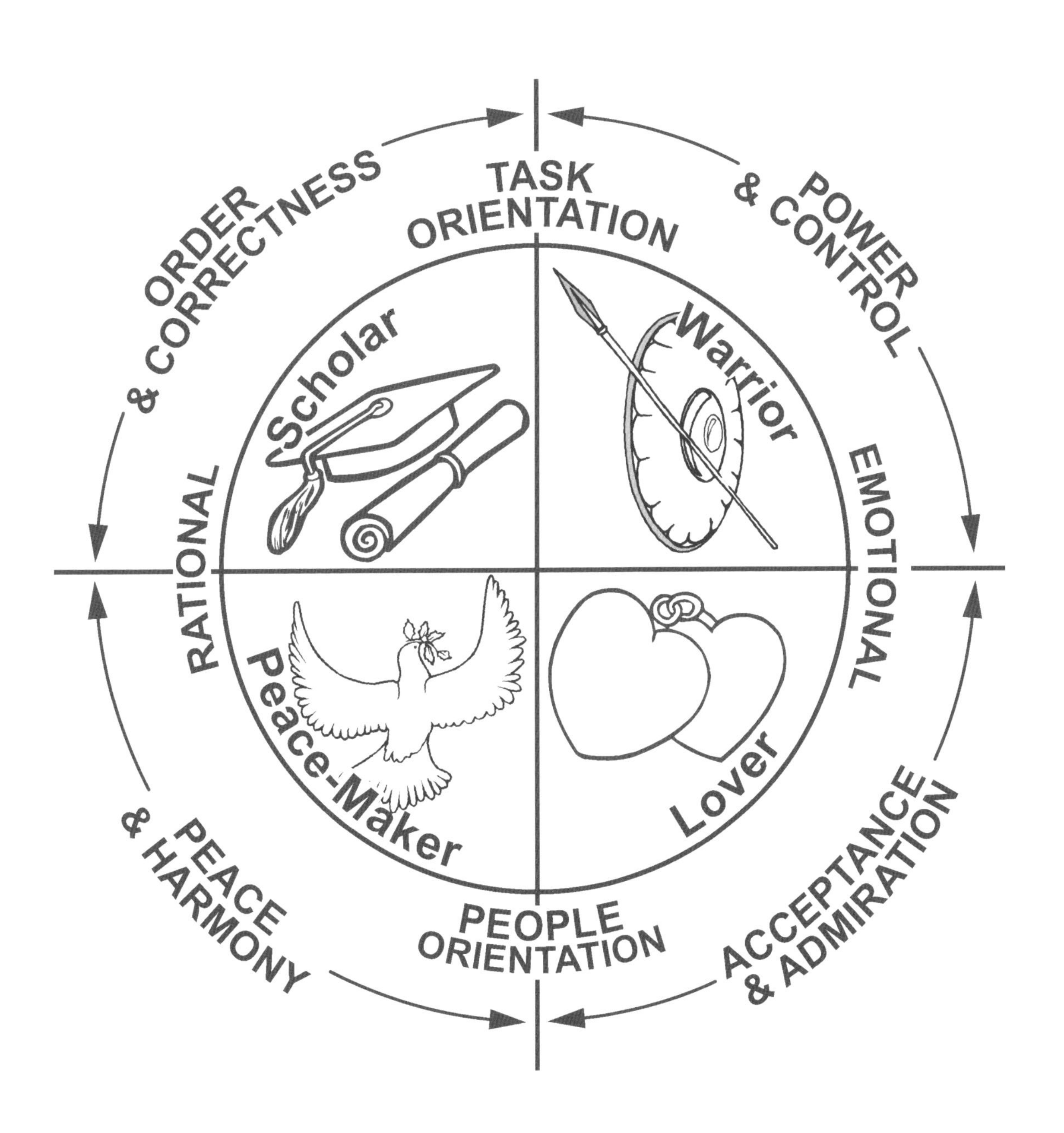

Temperament Questionnaire Instructions

Directions:

- ✔ For each personality trait score yourself from 0 (not like you) to 5 (like you). Don't hesitate to mark 5 if the trait fits you well (or 0 if it does not).
- ✔ Transfer your scores to the *TECHSTAR* Personality Scorecard.
- ✔ Color the center section of the Scorecard in accordance with the color legend.
- ✔ Shade each pie-section with the appropriate color to match your score.
- ✔ Add and record the quadrant scores (1-9, 10-18, 19-27, and 28-36) to determine which quadrants describe the strongest parts of your personality.
- ✔ Add and record the hemispherical scores (1-18, 10-27, 19-36, 28-9) to determine your tendencies toward task orientation (28-9) or people orientation (10-27), emotional orientation (1-18) or rational orientation (19-36).
- ✔ Consider having someone who knows you well score you and discuss the differences in their perceptions of your personality versus your own.

Temperament Questionnaire

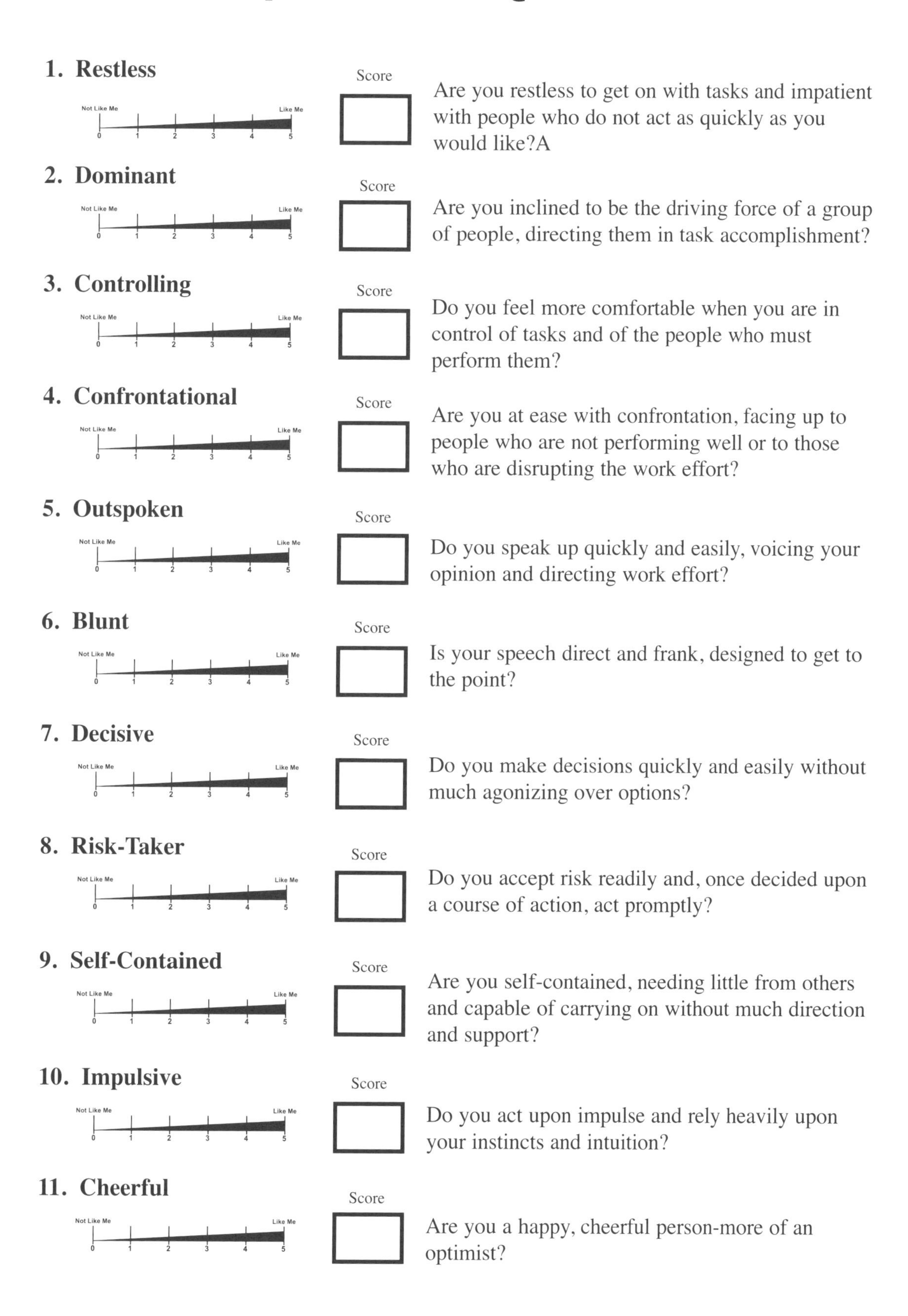

1. Restless

Not Like Me 0 1 2 3 4 5 Like Me

Score

Are you restless to get on with tasks and impatient with people who do not act as quickly as you would like?A

2. Dominant

Not Like Me 0 1 2 3 4 5 Like Me

Score

Are you inclined to be the driving force of a group of people, directing them in task accomplishment?

3. Controlling

Not Like Me 0 1 2 3 4 5 Like Me

Score

Do you feel more comfortable when you are in control of tasks and of the people who must perform them?

4. Confrontational

Not Like Me 0 1 2 3 4 5 Like Me

Score

Are you at ease with confrontation, facing up to people who are not performing well or to those who are disrupting the work effort?

5. Outspoken

Not Like Me 0 1 2 3 4 5 Like Me

Score

Do you speak up quickly and easily, voicing your opinion and directing work effort?

6. Blunt

Not Like Me 0 1 2 3 4 5 Like Me

Score

Is your speech direct and frank, designed to get to the point?

7. Decisive

Not Like Me 0 1 2 3 4 5 Like Me

Score

Do you make decisions quickly and easily without much agonizing over options?

8. Risk-Taker

Not Like Me 0 1 2 3 4 5 Like Me

Score

Do you accept risk readily and, once decided upon a course of action, act promptly?

9. Self-Contained

Not Like Me 0 1 2 3 4 5 Like Me

Score

Are you self-contained, needing little from others and capable of carrying on without much direction and support?

10. Impulsive

Not Like Me 0 1 2 3 4 5 Like Me

Score

Do you act upon impulse and rely heavily upon your instincts and intuition?

11. Cheerful

Not Like Me 0 1 2 3 4 5 Like Me

Score

Are you a happy, cheerful person-more of an optimist?

Temperament Questionnaire

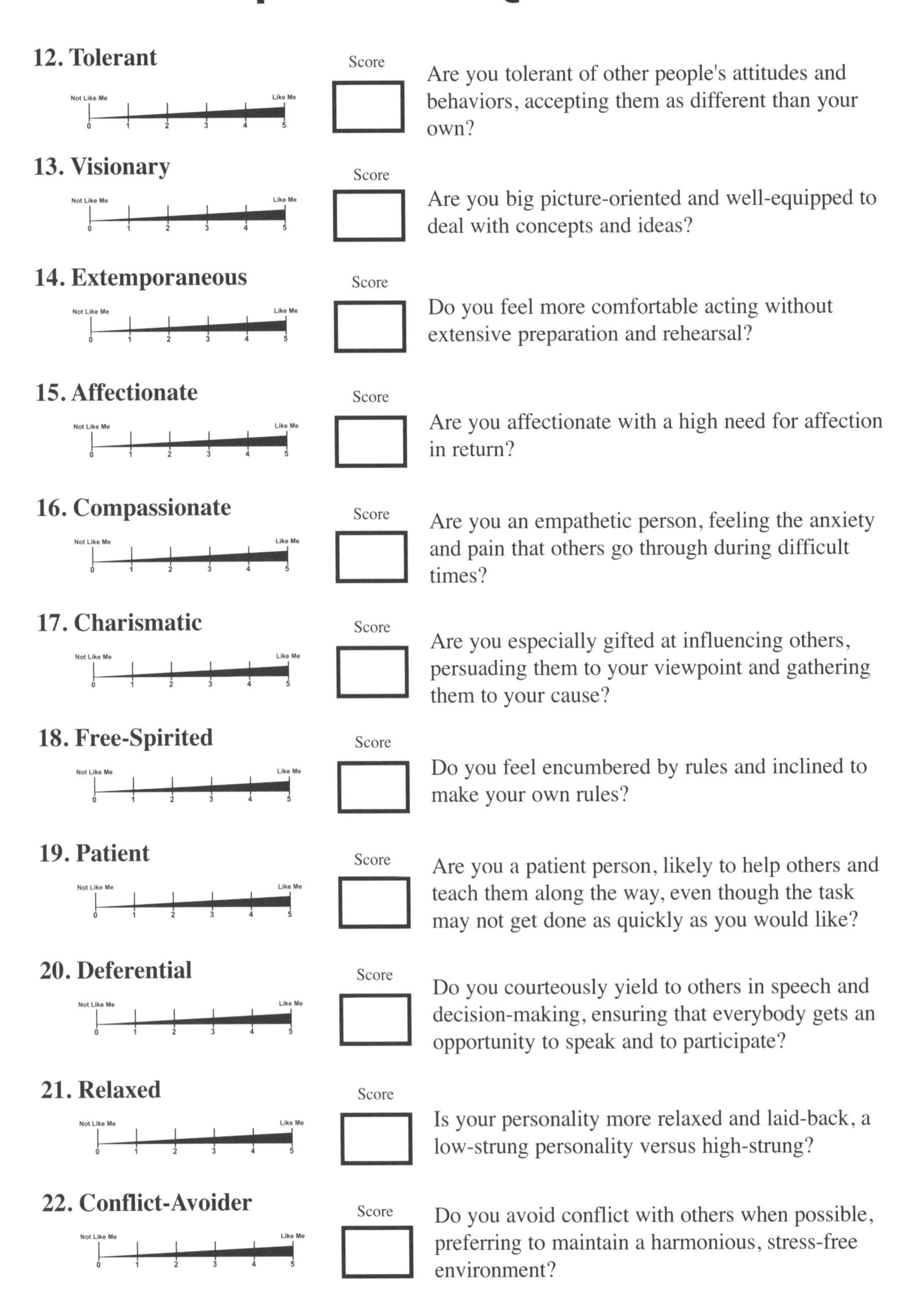

12. Tolerant

Not Like Me 0 1 2 3 4 5 Like Me

Score

Are you tolerant of other people's attitudes and behaviors, accepting them as different than your own?

13. Visionary

Not Like Me 0 1 2 3 4 5 Like Me

Score

Are you big picture-oriented and well-equipped to deal with concepts and ideas?

14. Extemporaneous

Not Like Me 0 1 2 3 4 5 Like Me

Score

Do you feel more comfortable acting without extensive preparation and rehearsal?

15. Affectionate

Not Like Me 0 1 2 3 4 5 Like Me

Score

Are you affectionate with a high need for affection in return?

16. Compassionate

Not Like Me 0 1 2 3 4 5 Like Me

Score

Are you an empathetic person, feeling the anxiety and pain that others go through during difficult times?

17. Charismatic

Not Like Me 0 1 2 3 4 5 Like Me

Score

Are you especially gifted at influencing others, persuading them to your viewpoint and gathering them to your cause?

18. Free-Spirited

Not Like Me 0 1 2 3 4 5 Like Me

Score

Do you feel encumbered by rules and inclined to make your own rules?

19. Patient

Not Like Me 0 1 2 3 4 5 Like Me

Score

Are you a patient person, likely to help others and teach them along the way, even though the task may not get done as quickly as you would like?

20. Deferential

Not Like Me 0 1 2 3 4 5 Like Me

Score

Do you courteously yield to others in speech and decision-making, ensuring that everybody gets an opportunity to speak and to participate?

21. Relaxed

Not Like Me 0 1 2 3 4 5 Like Me

Score

Is your personality more relaxed and laid-back, a low-strung personality versus high-strung?

22. Conflict-Avoider

Not Like Me 0 1 2 3 4 5 Like Me

Score

Do you avoid conflict with others when possible, preferring to maintain a harmonious, stress-free environment?

Temperament Questionnaire

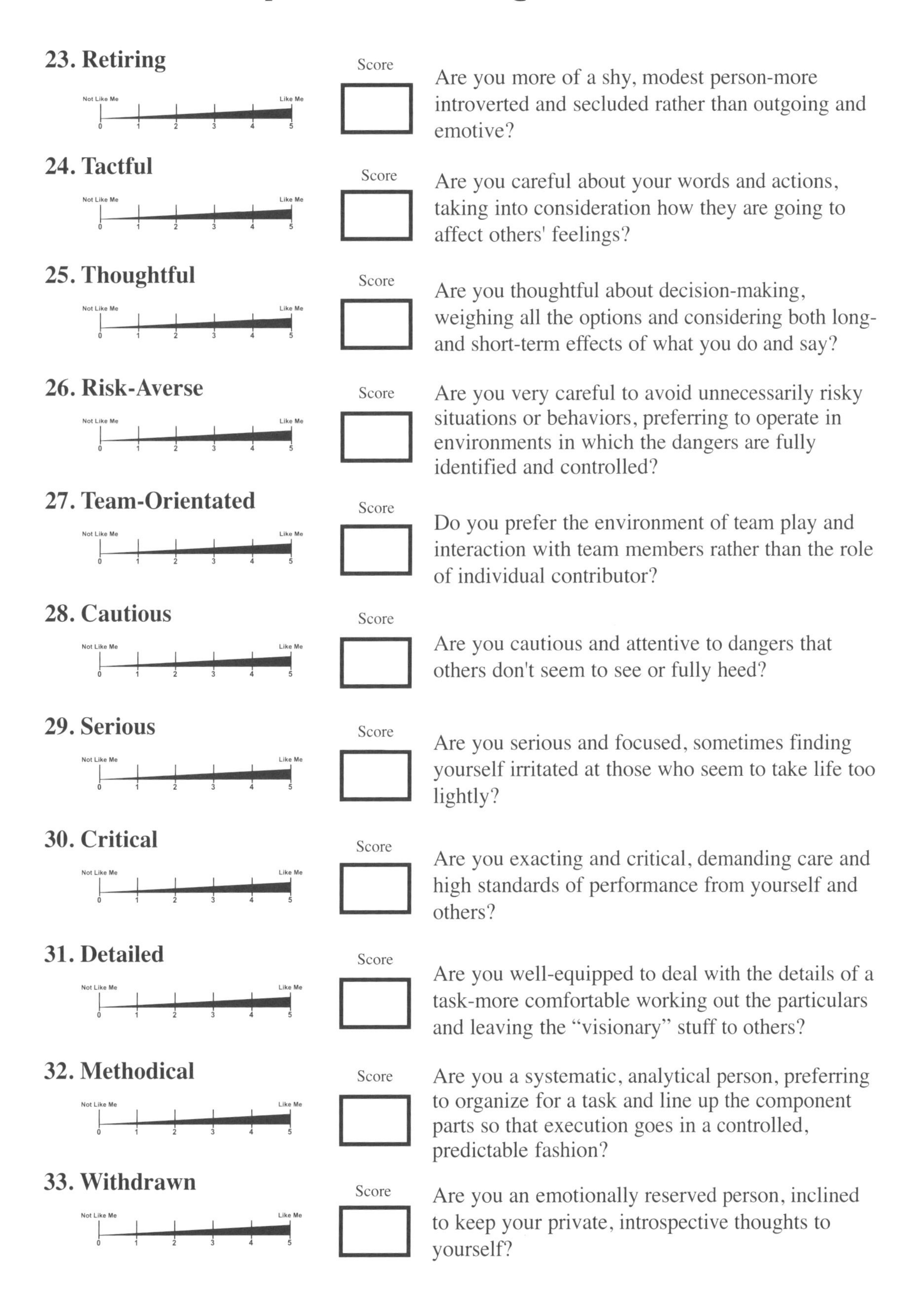

23. Retiring

Not Like Me 0 1 2 3 4 5 Like Me

Score

Are you more of a shy, modest person-more introverted and secluded rather than outgoing and emotive?

24. Tactful

Not Like Me 0 1 2 3 4 5 Like Me

Score

Are you careful about your words and actions, taking into consideration how they are going to affect others' feelings?

25. Thoughtful

Not Like Me 0 1 2 3 4 5 Like Me

Score

Are you thoughtful about decision-making, weighing all the options and considering both long- and short-term effects of what you do and say?

26. Risk-Averse

Not Like Me 0 1 2 3 4 5 Like Me

Score

Are you very careful to avoid unnecessarily risky situations or behaviors, preferring to operate in environments in which the dangers are fully identified and controlled?

27. Team-Orientated

Not Like Me 0 1 2 3 4 5 Like Me

Score

Do you prefer the environment of team play and interaction with team members rather than the role of individual contributor?

28. Cautious

Not Like Me 0 1 2 3 4 5 Like Me

Score

Are you cautious and attentive to dangers that others don't seem to see or fully heed?

29. Serious

Not Like Me 0 1 2 3 4 5 Like Me

Score

Are you serious and focused, sometimes finding yourself irritated at those who seem to take life too lightly?

30. Critical

Not Like Me 0 1 2 3 4 5 Like Me

Score

Are you exacting and critical, demanding care and high standards of performance from yourself and others?

31. Detailed

Not Like Me 0 1 2 3 4 5 Like Me

Score

Are you well-equipped to deal with the details of a task-more comfortable working out the particulars and leaving the "visionary" stuff to others?

32. Methodical

Not Like Me 0 1 2 3 4 5 Like Me

Score

Are you a systematic, analytical person, preferring to organize for a task and line up the component parts so that execution goes in a controlled, predictable fashion?

33. Withdrawn

Not Like Me 0 1 2 3 4 5 Like Me

Score

Are you an emotionally reserved person, inclined to keep your private, introspective thoughts to yourself?

Temperament Questionnaire

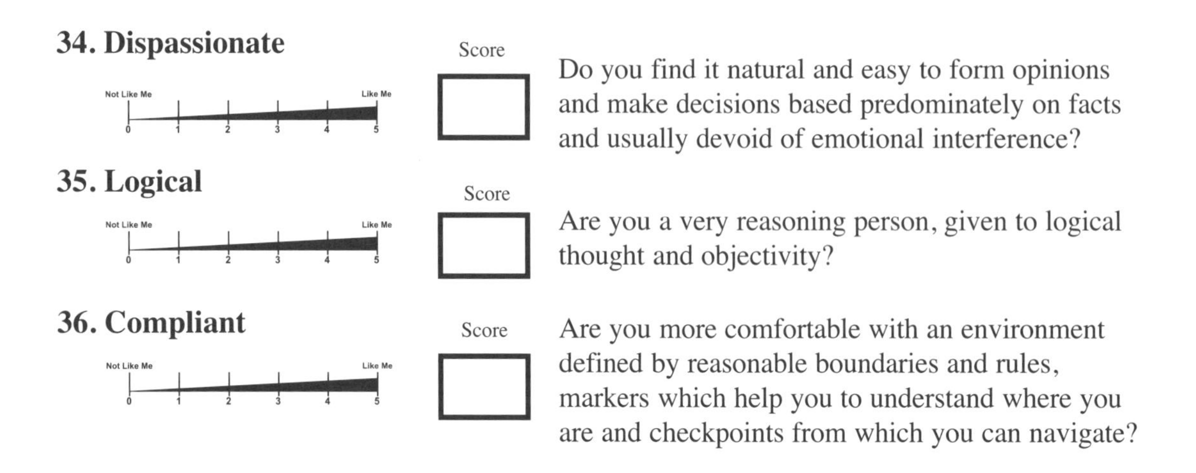

34. Dispassionate

Do you find it natural and easy to form opinions and make decisions based predominately on facts and usually devoid of emotional interference?

35. Logical

Are you a very reasoning person, given to logical thought and objectivity?

36. Compliant

Are you more comfortable with an environment defined by reasonable boundaries and rules, markers which help you to understand where you are and checkpoints from which you can navigate?

TECHSTAR Personality Scorecard

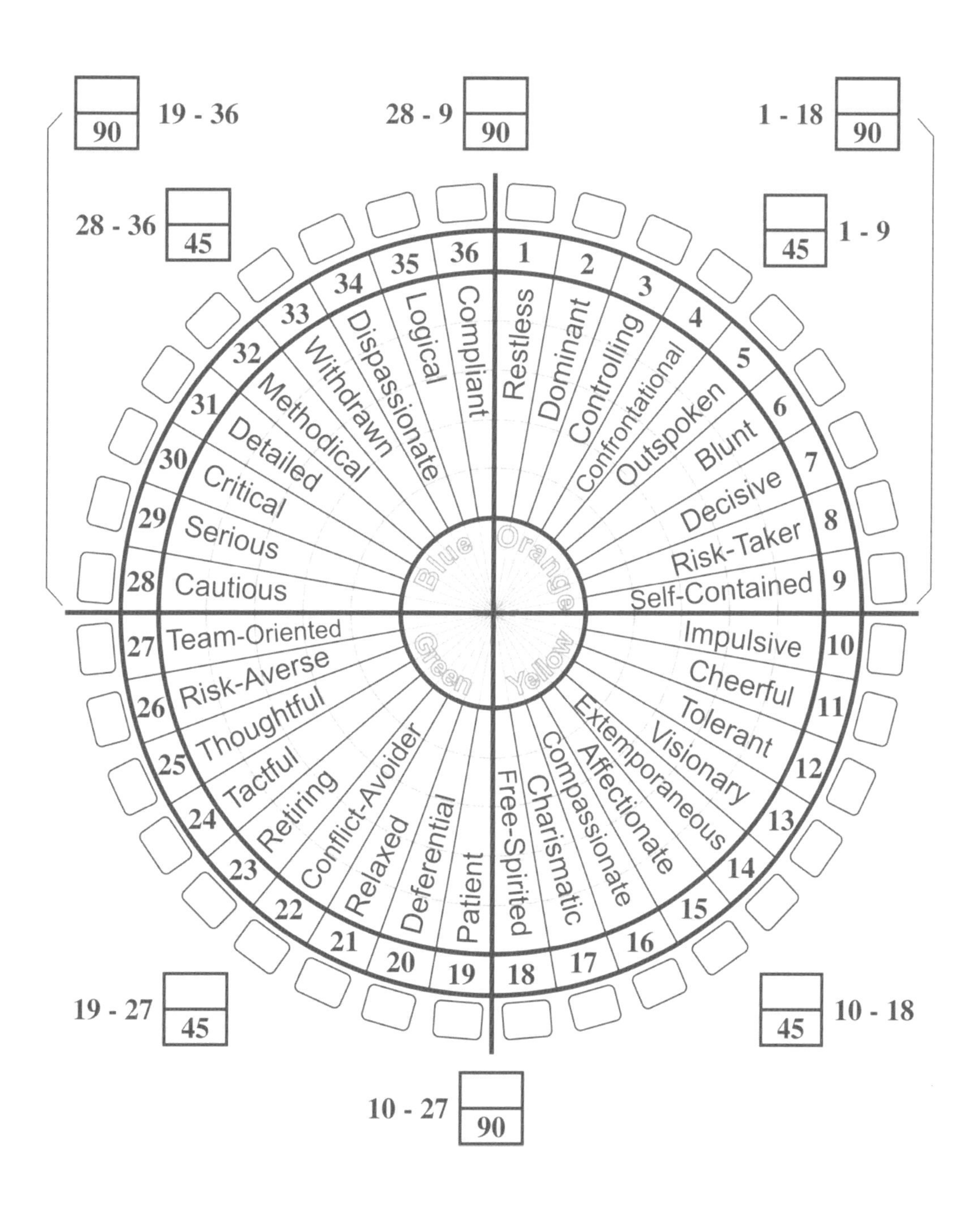

APPENDIX B

Leading Principles Summary

1. A MATTER OF TRUST

The basis of a leader's power and influence rests upon the leader's credibility. When a leader demonstrates characteristics, abilities, or behaviors that enhance his or her credibility in the eyes of team members, that leader's influence also increases. Conversely, when a leader's actions, behaviors, or demonstrated inabilities undermine his or her credibility, the leader's influence and power are diminished. Team members lose trust in leaders who are inept at directing the team's efforts or who are not forthright in dealing with people.

2. CHARACTER: THE FOUNDATION OF TRUST

A leader's character is a giant factor in his or her ability to lead. High character inspires trust and confidence and sets a standard of behavior for other team members. A leader's character is tested by moral and ethical dilemmas, especially when the outcome of the decision might be hidden.

3. ADVERSITY: THE FORGE OF CHARACTER

No person (nor any team) can ever become strong without facing and overcoming adversity. Just as the labor of exercise builds muscle, it is through overcoming hardship and solving difficult problems that individual and team character are constructed. The attitude with which leaders face adversity is a critical indicator of whether those leaders will succeed.

4. HONESTY: THE CORNERSTONE OF CHARACTER

Honesty is the quality of truthfulness of a leader. It is defamed by lies, broken promises, and duplicitous dealings with people. It begins with a conscience for serving others rather than self. (Is not dishonesty usually rooted in a selfish motive?) Honesty is demonstrated in each interaction with each person. It cannot be turned on or off at will. A leader with a reputation for dishonesty in the community is unlikely to obtain the respect and trust of a team at work.

5. TECHNICAL COMPETENCE: A QUALIFICATION FOR COACHING

Technical knowledge and skill are the bases upon which expertise power are built. Without them, leaders cannot fulfill the mentor role, cannot make wise decisions, and cannot effectively build and develop teams. In other words, it's impossible for incompetents to coach successfully.

6. INSPIRATION: BREATHING LIFE INTO THE TEAM

Pushes are sometimes necessary, especially in the training phases of teams, but, at the heart of leadership is the ability to inspire team members. It's what Lombardi meant when he said that real leaders get inside their people and motivate them.

7. VISIBILITY: A LEADER I CAN SEE

Teams need the reassurance of a present and visible coach, a competent leader to whom they can look for guidance, support, and courage, especially during difficult times. It is that very visibility which allows a leader to lead by personal example—transmitting values through conduct, language, dress, emotional control, humor, and resoluteness.

8. UNSELFISHNESS: A TEAM-SERVING ATTITUDE

Unselfish, team-serving behavior is a difficult leadership characteristic to learn. Leadership is, by nature, an exercise in the use of power. It's easy to become intoxicated with power. (Remember Lord Acton's admonition? *Power corrupts; absolute power corrupts absolutely*.) But egotistical leadership is a road to unwise decisions, poor judgment, and unclear thinking. There is no room for this on any team. The behavior and attitude of a leader greatly influences team members to act in a similar manner. It is imperative then that leaders set the example for unselfish thinking and behavior. One way that leaders can demonstrate unselfish behavior is by giving credit to others (and taking the blame when things go wrong). It is a sure sign of confidence and maturity in the character of a leader. When you practice this principle, you will be rewarded with the loyalty of your team.

9. HUMILITY: MODESTY OF SPIRIT

Arrogance is an unmistakable earmark of egotism. Arrogant leaders too often think of themselves before they think of the team. Humble leaders, on the other hand, focus on the team first. Because they are team-centered instead of self-centered, they can admit when they're wrong and laugh at themselves. Team members typically view them as human and compassionate, not as conceited and disdainful. As a result, they are usually respected leaders.

10. COMMUNICATION: PAINTING CLEAR PICTURES

Teamwork is impossible without effective communication. It is through communication that teammates learn values, share ideas, set goals, and obtain the perspective for resolving problems. It is essential, then, that leaders be communicative. But, a leader does not have to be extroverted to effectively communicate. In fact quiet, listening leaders are better for some organizations and some situations. The key is not how loudly the message is delivered, but rather its clarity and persuasiveness. Remember, Mr. Lincoln, though friendly, was not extroverted. Yet, by painting into the minds of his listeners the pictures that were in his own mind, he was one of the most effective communicators of the 19th Century.

11. JUSTNESS: A FAIR AND OBJECTIVE VIEW

Prejudicial behavior (making judgments in the absence of fact), unfair dealings with peers and subordinates, and unreasonable demands are all destructive behaviors that destroy the credibility and effectiveness of leaders. Conversely, objectivity, fairness, and circumspect dealings create a climate of respect and openness, the climate in which complex problems are more likely to be solved.

12. CONSISTENCY: WALKING THE TALK

The characteristics of integrity and consistency tell team members that their leader is “whole or undivided” in thinking and that they can expect “logical coherence” in behavior and standards. Such leaders don't just talk standards and practices. They live them as well. Such behavior tends to inspire trust and commitment, two important ingredients in the concoction of a team.

13. RESPECT: A TWO-WAY STREET

Though team members are (or, at least, should be) bound to respect a leader's position, they are not bound to respect the leader. Personal respect is earned through fair and respectful dealings with team members, proof of professional competence, and professional demeanor.

14. DECISIVENESS: SOMEONE HAS TO MAKE CHOICES

Decisiveness describes the ability of a leader to make decisions in a timely manner based upon the information that is reasonably available. Decisiveness should not be confused with good judgment. Fast decisions are not necessarily good decisions. Similarly, delayed decisions can often be disastrous. Good judgment must always temper decisiveness.

15. LOYALTY: KEEPING FAITH WITH THE TEAM

Loyalty is the quality of faithfulness to a person, an organization, a country, or a cause. Loyalty, as all other leadership characteristics, is contagious. Conversely, disloyalty will destroy a fundamentally good organization rapidly. Loyalty holds a team together when difficulties try to tear it apart. It is a product of trust, born of forthright, just dealings with one another. Loyalty is a two-way street. If I want loyalty from my team, I must demonstrate loyalty to my team.

16. COURAGE: COMMITMENT TO DO RIGHT

Courage is the quality of character which allows one to face danger, not without fear, but with the resoluteness and confidence that comes from doing what is right. It may be displayed physically or morally. Physical courage is not often required in the modern business world, but moral courage is. Moral courage describes the propensity of a leader to make decisions based upon principle rather than upon special interest pressures or personal biases (even if the leader stands to lose personally by such action). A leader lacking moral courage is likely to be unethical, since doing the right thing is often difficult.

17. UNDERSTANDING YOUR ROLE

Leaders are the structural center of a team, the hub around which the organizational wheel is built. Leaders forge motivated team members into a synergistic being that is stronger by far than all of the members separately. Leaders demonstrate the behaviors and attitudes that they expect of each team member. And leaders release the energy of their teams at the right times and for the right purposes for accomplishing objectives.

18. KNOWING YOURSELF

Personality is the image of a leader, a picture of human qualities etched into the minds of team members. If the image is genuine, not feigned or contrived, the words and actions of the leader are far more believable. So, be yourself! If God made you an outgoing person, be a good outgoing leader. If He crafted you as a quiet person, then be a good quiet leader.

19. MOTIVATING THE TEAM

Have-to motivation and *want-to* motivation are both legitimate tools. But they have very different purposes. The former is a turning tool. The latter is the only tool that can ultimately take you and your team to Olympic-level performance. Great leaders know how and when to use each tool.

20. BALANCING PEOPLE AND PRODUCTION

Leaders must perpetually push their teams toward higher standards of performance while, at the same time, reassuring them of the probability of success through training, coaching and encouragement, forces that seem to pull in opposite directions. It is the resolution of these two forces that leads to superior performance.

21. CARING FOR THE TEAM

When leaders demonstrate that they care about their subordinates, a strong bond of affinity develops. It is the platform upon which the strongest form of organizational influence—personal power—is constructed. It forms the basis of trust, without which a team cannot grow beyond mediocrity.

22. USING POWER AND INFLUENCE

Power is a measure of a leader's ability to influence the members of a team toward accomplishment of a goal. It is the currency of leadership; and, like money, it is neither good nor evil. It is a commodity that may be used for proper purposes or improper ends. Wise leaders accumulate power in all of its forms and learn to select the proper form to address each problem. Like a master carpenter, a wise leader has a toolbox full of tools and the ability to employ each for its intended purpose.

23. NAVIGATING THE CORPORATE TERRAIN

Leading a corporate team along a business path is a lot like navigating in the wilderness. You need to know where you want to go, where you are, and what intermediate objectives you need to reach in order to achieve your end destination. Route-finding becomes easier when team members participate in determining the intermediate objectives and remain constantly aware of direction and current location.

24. DISCIPLINING THE TEAM

Discipline is the process of instructing, training, encouraging, persuading, exhorting, praising, reprimanding, and sometimes punishing those over whom we have authority (and for whom we bear responsibility) toward individual and team development for the purpose of accomplishing a mission. The primary purpose of discipline is to forge the raw material of individual team members into an implement more powerful than any single team member.

25. ENCOURAGING CRITICISM

No one (nor any team) improves without constructive criticism. All good coaches know that they must observe, evaluate, and provide feedback to their players if they expect the team to make positive changes. Yet, few people enjoy being criticized. Therefore, successful leaders learn to provide criticism in a way that's "hearable". Further, good leaders teach players how to coach one another and how to provide constructive feedback to their coaches as well.

26. A TEAM APPROACH

Great accomplishments are nearly always the result of a team approach. Consequently, to be effective, leaders must be team-forgers, assembling the components of a team and molding them into synergistic units capable of accomplishing far more than the sum of uncoordinated individual efforts.

27. INGREDIENTS OF A TEAM

Besides leaders and team members, teams need a clear mission, an efficient team structure, open lines of communication, reasonable rules of play, an effective and continuous training regimen, and a means to evaluate player and team performance.

28. STEPS IN BUILDING A TEAM

Learning to lead is a lifelong experience. Fortunately, the lessons of leadership are neither mysterious nor obscure. The characteristics of great leaders are written in the pages of history for any who are willing to study it. Great leaders are distinguished by shared traits, skills, and principles which may be analyzed and learned.

29. CHARACTERISTICS OF GOOD TEAM MEMBERS

Even the best leaders can't teach anything to team members who are unwilling to learn. A teachable attitude is a vital characteristic of a team player.

30. THE TEAM FEELING

When a team learns how to win and what it feels like to win, winning becomes easier. Team members begin to realize that the team can accomplish more working together than all the players working independently.

APPENDIX C

Trust-Breaker Summary

WE DON'T WILLINGLY FOLLOW LEADERS WHO...

ARE NOT TRUSTWORTHY • ARE OF UNSOUND CHARACTER • CAN'T HANDLE DIFFICULTY • LIE TO US • AREN'T TECHNICALLY COMPETENT • LEAVE US LIFELESS • ARE NOT VISIBLE • ARE SELF-SERVING INSTEAD OF TEAM-SERVING • SEEM OVERLY IMPRESSED WITH THEIR OWN IMPORTANCE • CAN'T EXPLAIN WHAT THEY WANT US TO DO • AREN'T FAIR • SAY ONE THING AND DO ANOTHER • TREAT US DISRESPECTFULLY • CAN'T MAKE UP THEIR OWN MINDS • DON'T SUPPORT US • WON'T TAKE A STAND • DON'T KNOW THEIR PURPOSE • DON'T KNOW THEMSELVES • DON'T UNDERSTAND US • DON'T CHALLENGE US • DON'T CARE FOR US • MISUSE POWER • ARE POOR ROUTE-FINDERS • DON'T UNDERSTAND THE MEANING OF DISCIPLINE • DON'T TELL US HOW WE ARE DOING • DON'T FOSTER TEAMWORK • DON'T UNDERSTAND THE INGREDIENTS OF A TEAM • DON'T KNOW THE STEPS IN TEAM BUILDING • DON'T ENGENDER A FEELING OF ESPRIT WITHIN THE TEAM

END NOTES

INTRODUCTION.

1. George S. Patton, Jr. *Success in War.* 1931.
2. Pat Riley. *The Winner Within: A Life Plane for Team Players* (New York: Riles & Company, Inc., 1993), 15.

Chapter 2. CHARACTER: A FOUNDATION FOR TRUST

1. Charles Bracelen Flood. *Lee: The Last Year* (Boston: Houghton Mifflin Company, 1981), 16.
2. Tom Landry with Greg Lewis. *Tom Landry: An Autobiography* (Grand Rapids: Zondervan Publishing House; New York: HarperCollins*Publishers,* 1990), 292.
3. Tom Landry with Greg Lewis. *Tom Landry: An Autobiography* (Grand Rapids: Zondervan Publishing House; New York: HarperCollins*Publishers,* 1990), 292.
4. Margaret Thatcher. *Talking with David Frost: Margaret Thatcher* (Washington, DC: David Paradine Television and WETA, 1991).
5. Oren Harari. *The Leadership Secrets of Colin Powell* (New York: McGraw-Hill, 2002), 255.
6. Oren Harari. *The Leadership Secrets of Colin Powell* (New York: McGraw-Hill, 2002), 255-256.
7. John C. Maxwell. *Your Attitude: Key to Success* (San Bernardino: Here's Life Publishers, Inc., 1984), 32.

Chapter 3. ADVERSITY: THE FORGE OF CHARACTER

1. Tom Landry with Greg Lewis. *Tom Landry: An Autobiography* (Grand Rapids: Zondervan Publishing House; New York: HarperCollins*Publishers,* 1990), 286.
2. Viktor E. Frankl. *Man's Search for Meaning* (New York: Simon & Schuster Inc., 1984), 88.
3. Viktor E. Frankl. *Man's Search for Meaning* (New York: Simon & Schuster Inc., 1984), 98.
4. M. Scott Peck, M.D. *The Road Less Traveled: A New Psychology of Love, Traditional Values and Spiritual Growth* (New York: Touchstone, 2003), 15.

Chapter 4. HONESTY: THE CORNERSTONE OF CHARACTER

1. Fyodor Dostoevsky. *The Brothers Karamazov.*

Chapter 5. TECHNICAL COMPETENCE: A QUALIFICATION FOR COACHING

1. Hyman Rickover. *Hearings Before the Subcommittee on Energy Research and Production of the Committee on Science and Technology,* U.S. House of Representatives, Ninety-Sixth Congress, May 22, 23, 24, 1979 (Washington, D.C.: U.S. Government Printing Office, 1979), 889-890.
2. George S. Patton, Jr. *Success in War*

Chapter 6. INSPIRATION: BREATHING LIFE INTO THE TEAM

1. Carlo D'Este. *Patton: A Genius for War* (New York: HarperCollins*Publishers,* 1995), 433.
2. George S. Patton, Jr. *War As I Knew It* (Boston: Houghton Mifflin Company, 1975), 288.

Chapter 8. UNSELFISHNESS: A TEAM-SERVING ATTITUDE

1. George S. Patton, Jr. *War As I Knew It* (Boston: Houghton Mifflin Company, 1975), 274.
2. Geoffrey Perret. *Eisenhower* (Holbrook: Adams Media Corporation, 1999), 325.
3. Andrew Hill with John Wooden. *Be Quick-But Don't Hurry! Finding Success in the Teachings of a Lifetime* (New York: Simon & Schuster, Inc., 2001), 111.
4. Andrew Hill with John Wooden. *Be Quick-But Don't Hurry! Finding Success in the Teachings of a Lifetime* (New York: Simon & Schuster, Inc., 2001), 112-113.

End Notes

Chapter 9. HUMILITY: MODESTY OF SPIRIT

1. Mike McKinley. "SecNav Challenges Navy's Leaders," in *All Hands* Magazine, February, 1988, 14-15.

Chapter 10. COMMUNICATION: PAINTING CLEAR PICTURES

1. George S. Patton, Jr. *War As I Knew It* (Boston: Houghton Mifflin Company, 1975), 275.
2. George S. Patton, Jr. *War As I Knew It* (Boston: Houghton Mifflin Company, 1975), 310.

Chapter 12. CONSISTENCY: WALKING THE TALK

1. Joe Paterno with Bernard Asbell. *Paterno: By the Book* (New York: Random House, Inc., 1989), 84.

Chapter 14: DECISIVENESS: SOMEONE HAS TO MAKE CHOICES

1. George S. Patton, Jr. *War As I Knew It* (Boston: Houghton Mifflin Company, 1975), 273.

Chapter 15: LOYALTY: KEEPING FAITH WITH THE TEAM

1. George S. Patton, Jr. *War As I Knew It* (Boston: Houghton Mifflin Company, 1975), 281.

Chapter 16: COURAGE: COMMITMENT TO DO RIGHT

1. George S. Patton, Jr. *War As I Knew It* (Boston: Houghton Mifflin Company, 1975), 262-263.

Chapter 17: UNDERSTANDING YOUR ROLE

1. Bill Parcells with Jeff Coplon. *Finding a Way to Win: The Principles of Leadership, Teamwork, and Motivation* (New York: Bantam Doubleday Dell Publishing Group, Inc., 1995), 8.
2. Mike McKinley. "SecNav Challenges Navy's Leaders," in *All Hands* Magazine, February, 1988, 14.
3. Robert Townsend. *Further Up the Organization* (New York: Harper & Row, Publishers, Inc., 1984), 169.
4. Ben R. Rich and Leo Janos. *Skunk Works: A Personal Memoir of My Years at Lockheed* (Boston: Little, Brown and Company, 1994), 337-338.
5. Tom Landry with Greg Lewis. *Tom Landry: An Autobiography* (Grand Rapids: Zondervan Publishing House; New York: HarperCollins*Publishers*, 1990), 276.
6. Mary Walton. *The Deming Management Method* (New York: The Putnam Publishing Group, 1986), 35.

Chapter 18. KNOWING YOURSELF

1. *The Excellence Files* (Cambridge: Enterprise Media and Scott/Tyler Productions, 1997). A video interview with Herb Kelleher.
2. Joe Paterno with Bernard Asbell. *Paterno: By the Book* (New York: Random House, Inc., 1989), 84.
3. David Keirsey. *Please Understand Me II: Temperament, Character, Intelligence* (Del Mar, CA: Prometheus Nemesis Book Company, 1998), 13.
4. DiSC: *Dimensions of Behavior,* "Personal Profile System, 2800 Series" (Minneapolis: Inscape Publishing, Inc., 2001), 7.
5. Sun Tzu. *Sun Tzu: The Art of War* Translated by Samuel B. Griffith (New York: Oxford University Press, 1971), 84.

END NOTES

Chapter 19. MOTIVATING THE TEAM

1. Tom Landry with Greg Lewis. *Tom Landry: An Autobiography* (Grand Rapids: Zondervan Publishing House; New York: HarperCollins*Publishers,* 1990), 284.
2. Tom Landry with Greg Lewis. *Tom Landry: An Autobiography* (Grand Rapids: Zondervan Publishing House; New York: HarperCollins*Publishers,* 1990), 284.
3. Carlo D'Este. *Patton: A Genius for War* (New York: HarperCollins*Publishers,* 1995), 462.
4. Douglas Southall Freeman. *Lee: An Abridgement* (New York: Charles Scribner's Sons, 1961), 510.
5. Abraham Lincoln. *Abraham Lincoln in His Own Words* (New York: Barnes & Noble Books, 1996), 73-74.
6. David Satter. "Why Russia Can't Feed Itself, in *Reader's Digest* (Pleasantville, NY: Reader's Digest Association, Inc., Oct, 1989), 61-66.

Chapter 20: BALANCING PEOPLE AND PRODUCTION

1. Robert R. Blake and Jane Srygley Mouton. *The New Managerial Grid* (Houston: Gulf Publishing Company, 1978), 11.
2. Phillip Zimbardo. "The Power of the Situation," *Discovering Psychology* (S. Burlington: The Annenberg/CPB Collection, 1989). From the video series *Discovering Psychology.*

Chapter 21. CARING FOR THE TEAM

1. George S. Patton, Jr. *War As I Knew It* (Boston: Houghton Mifflin Company, 1975), 308-309.
2. Kenneth H. Blanchard and Spencer Johnson. *The One Minute Manager* (William Morrow and Company, Inc., 1983), 34, 44.
3. Joe Paterno with Bernard Asbell. *Paterno: By the Book* (New York: Random House, Inc., 1989), 81.
4. Joe Paterno with Bernard Asbell. *Paterno: By the Book* (New York: Random House, Inc., 1989), 82-83.
5. John C. Maxwell. *Your Attitude: Key to Success* (San Bernardino: Here's Life Publishers, Inc., 1984), 49.
6. Mike Shanahan with Adam Schefter. *Think Like a Champion: Building Success One Victory at a Time* (New York: HarperCollins*Publishers,* 1999), 52.
7. Andrew Hill with John Wooden. *Be Quick-But Don't Hurry! Finding Success in the Teachings of a Lifetime* (New York: Simon & Schuster, Inc., 2001), 105.
8. Chang Yu. *Sun Tzu: The Art of War* translated by Samuel B. Griffith (New York: Oxford University Press, 1971), 64.
9. George S. Patton, Jr. *War As I Knew It* (Boston: Houghton Mifflin Company, 1975), 273-274.
10. Tom Peters and Nancy Austin. *A Passion for Excellence: The Leadership Difference* (New York: Warner Books, Inc., 1986), 343.
11. Tom Peters and Nancy Austin. *A Passion for Excellence: The Leadership Difference* (New York: Warner Books, Inc., 1986), 240.

Chapter 22. USING POWER AND INFLUENCE

1. TuMu. *Sun Tzu: The Art of War* Translated by Samuel B. Griffith (New York: Oxford University Press, 1971), 65.
2. Tom Landry with Greg Lewis. *Tom Landry: An Autobiography* (Grand Rapids: Zondervan Publishing House; New York: HarperCollins*Publishers,* 1990), 280.

END NOTES

3. Douglas Southall Freeman. *Lee: An Abridgement* (New York: Charles Scribner's Sons, 1961), 585.
4. Niccolo Machiavelli. *The Prince: A New Translation, Backgrounds, Interpretations* translated and edited by Robert M. Adams (New York: W.W. Norton & Company, Inc., 1977), 50.

Chapter 23: NAVIGATING THE CORPORATE TERRAIN

1. Tom Landry with Greg Lewis. *Tom Landry: An Autobiography* (Grand Rapids: Zondervan Publishing House; New York: HarperCollins*Publishers,* 1990), 272-273.
2. Mike Krzyzewski with Donald T. Phillips. *Leading with the Heart: Successful Strategies for Basketball, Business, and Life* (New York: Warner Books, Inc., 2000), 33-35.

Chapter 24. DISCIPLINING THE TEAM

1. Antoine Henri Jomini. Jomini: *The Art of War* (Westport, CT: Greenwood Press, Publishers, originally published in 1862), 38.
2. *The American Heritage Dictionary, 2nd College Edition* (Boston: Houghton Mifflin Company, 1985), 1233.
3. George S. Patton, Jr. *War As I Knew It* (Boston: Houghton Mifflin Company, 1975), 308, 313.
4. Joe Paterno with Bernard Asbell. *Paterno: By the Book* (New York: Random House, Inc., 1989), 81.

Chapter 25: ENCOURAGING CRITICISM

1. Pat Riley. *The Winner Within: A Life Plan for Team Players* (New York: Riles & Company, Inc., 1993), 144.
2. Tom Landry with Greg Lewis. *Tom Landry: An Autobiography* (Grand Rapids: Zondervan Publishing House; New York: HarperCollins*Publishers,* 1990), 287.
3. Dale Carnegie. *Lincoln the Unknown* (Garden City, NY: Dale Carnegie & Associates, 1959), 155.

Chapter 26: A TEAM APPROACH

1. Hyman Rickover. *Hearings Before the Subcommittee on Energy Research and Production of the Committee on Science and Technology, U.S. House of Representatives, Ninety-Eighth Congress, May 22, 1984* (Washington, D.C.: U.S. Government Printing Office, 1985), 231.

Chapter 28. STEPS IN BUILDING A TEAM

1. Joe Paterno with Bernard Asbell. *Paterno: By the Book* (New York: Random House, Inc., 1989), 84.

Chapter 29. CHARACTERISTICS OF GOOD TEAM MEMBERS

1. Joe Paterno with Bernard Asbell. *Paterno: By the Book* (New York: Random House, Inc., 1989), 272.

CONCLUSION

1. Abraham Lincoln. *Abraham Lincoln in His Own Words* (New York: Barnes & Noble Books, 1996), 251.

Helpful Books

A Passion for Excellence by Tom Peters and Nancy Austin
Churchill on Leadership by Steven F. Hayward
Deming Management at Work by Mary Walton
Emotional Intelligence by Daniel Goleman
Failure is Not an Option by Eugene Krantz
Further Up the Organization by Robert Townsend
Groupthink by Irving L. Janis
Hoover's FBI by Cartha D. "Deke" DeLoach
How to Win Friends and Influence People by Dale Carnegie
In Search of Excellence by Thomas J. Peters and Robert H. Waterman, Jr.
Leadership Secrets of Attila the Hun by Wess Roberts, Ph.D.
Lee: An Abridgement by Douglas Southall Freeman, abridged by Richard Harwell
Lee: The Last Years by Charles Bracelen Flood
Lincoln on Leadership by Don Phillips
Lincoln the Unknown by Dale Carnegie
Man's Search for Meaning by Viktor E. Frankl
Management of Organizational Behavior by Paul Hersey and Kenneth Blanchard
Marine! The Life of Chesty Puller by Burke Davis
My American Journey by Colin Powell
Old Soldiers Never Die by Geoffrey Perret
Paterno: By the Book by Joe Paterno with Bernard Asbell
Patton: A Genius for War by Carlo D'Este
Patton on Leadership by Alan Axelrod
Please Understand Me II by David Keirsey
Sam Walton: Made in America by Sam Walton with John Huey
Skunk Works by Ben R. Rich and Leo Janos
Son of the Morning Star by Evan S. Connell
Stonewall Jackson by G.F.R. Henderson
Sun Tzu: The Art of War translated by Samuel B. Griffith
The Caine Mutiny by Herman Wouk
The Deming Management Method by Mary Walton
The Effective Executive by Peter Drucker
The Hungry Ocean by Linda Greenlaw
The Killer Angels by Michael Shaara
The Leadership Secrets of Colin Powell by Oren Harari
The New Managerial Grid by Robert R. Blake and Jane S. Mouton
The One Minute Manager by Kenneth Blanchard and Spencer Johnson
The Renewal Factor by Robert H. Waterman, Jr.
The Rickover Effect by Theodore Rockwell
The Seven Habits of Highly Effective People by Steven R. Covey
The Seven Laws of Teaching by John Milton Gregory
The Winner Within by Pat Riley
Tom Landry: An Autobiography by Tom Landry with Gregg Lewis
Ulysses S. Grant: Soldier and President by Geoffrey Perret
Understanding the Male Temperament by Tim LaHaye
War as I Knew It by General George S. Patton, Jr.
When Pride Still Mattered by David Maraniss
Your Attitude: Key to Success by John C. Maxwell

HELPFUL FILMS

Apollo 13 1995 PG 140 min Universal Studios
Bridge on the River Kwai 1957 PG 161 min Columbia Pictures
Brubaker 1980 R 132 min Fox Home Entertainment
Butch Cassidy and the Sundance Kid 1969 PG 110 min Twentieth Century Fox
Coach Carter 2005 PG13 136 min Paramount Home Entertainment
Crimson Tide 1995 R 116 min Disney
Dangerous Minds 1995 R 99 min Hollywood Pictures
Gettysburg 1993 PG 261 min Warner Home Video
Glory Road 2006 PG 109 min Buena Vista Pictures
High Noon 1952 NR 85 min Lions Gate Home Entertainment
Hoosiers 1986 PG 115 min MGM/UA Studios
K-19: The Widowmaker 2002 PG-13 138 min Paramount Home Entertainment
Lean on Me 1989 PG-13 104 min Warner Studios
Miracle 2004 PG 135 min Buena Vista Home Video
Mrs. Brown 1997 PG 103 min Disney / Buena Vista
Mutiny on the Bounty 1935 NR 132 min Warner Home Video
Patton 1970 PG 172 min 20th Century Fox Home Entertainment
Remember the Titans 2000 PG 114 min Buena Vista Home Entertainment
Saving Private Ryan 1998 R 169 min Universal Studios Home Video
Shackleton 2002 NR 200 min New Video Group
Sister Act 1992 PG 100 min Buena Vista Home Entertainment
Stand and Deliver 1988 PG 103 min Warner Home Video
The Caine Mutiny 1954 NR 125 min Sony Pictures Home Entertainment
The Cowboys 1972 PG 135 min Warner Home Video
The Edge 1997 R 117 min
The Flight of the Phoenix 1965 NR 147 min 20th Century Fox Home Entertainment
The Hill 1965 NR 123 min MGM/UA Home Video
The Hunt for Red October 1990 PG 135 min Paramount Home Video
The Karate Kid 1984 PG 127 min Sony Pictures Home Entertainment
To Sir, With Love 1967 NR 105 min Sony Pictures Home Entertainment
Twelve O'Clock High 1949 NR 132 min 20th Century Fox Home Entertainment
12 Angry Men 1957 NR 96 min MGM Home Entertainment
We Were Soldiers 2002 R 138 min Paramount Home Video
White Squall 1996 PG-13 128 min Buena Vista Home Entertainment

INDEX

INDEX